TRANSFORMING CONGREGATIONAL CULTURE

TRANSFORMING CONGREGATIONAL CULTURE

Anthony B. Robinson

WILLIAM B. EERDMANS PUBLISHING COMPANY
GRAND RAPIDS, MICHIGAN / CAMBRIDGE, U.K.

Wm. B. Eerdmans Publishing Co.
255 Jefferson Ave. S.E., Grand Rapids, Michigan 49503 /
P.O. Box 163, Cambridge CB3 9PU U.K.

Printed in the United States of America

07 06 05 04 03   7 6 5 4 3 2 1

Library of Congress Cataloging-in-Publication Data

Robinson, Anthony B.
    Transforming congregational culture / Anthony B. Robinson.
        p.   cm.
    Includes index.
    ISBN 0-8028-0518-3 (pbk.: alk. paper)
    1. Church renewal.   I. Title.

  BV600.3 .R63   2003
  262′.001′7 — dc21

                                    2002035408

www.eerdmans.com

Contents

Introduction

Do we need yet another book on renewal and change in the mainline church? In recent years a kind of cottage industry has developed, turning out literature, workbooks, and conferences on the mainline church and what to do for it, about it, or with it. Some of this has been quite helpful.

I offer this contribution because in several respects it is, I hope, different from many of the others. For one thing, I am not a consultant; neither am I a guru, nor even an expert. I am a pastor. What I discuss here derives from my pastoral work and experience. The challenges and the changes I describe are not simply good ideas. They have been discovered, tested, trashed, redrawn, lived with, and lived out in actual congregations. The larger framework in which I locate them is derived from twenty-five years of pastoral ministry at a time of a great shift, of an enormous change and challenge, for mainline churches and denominations. I have gained that pastoral experience, I might add, chiefly in four quite different congregations — congregations that have provided me with quite different kinds of experiences. They have included small, medium, and large churches; urban, rural, and suburban settings; and ethnically homogeneous and multi-ethnic congregations.

Not only do these ideas emerge out of actual practice of ministry in a variety of congregational settings, but also my approach seeks to affirm and build on the best of the mainline Protestant experience while being very clear about the need for change. I do not take the position that all we have been or now are needs to be junked and we must all try to become conservative congregations or mega-churches. Change is required. And mainline congregations must do their work better than we have done it in recent years. But we have our own genius and heritage, and we will do better to discern and build on that than to regret it or deny it.

Another reason that I am bold to offer this book to the church and my colleagues in leadership is that I take an approach here that I describe as "cultural change." I will describe this in the second chapter, but for now I will say that technical or programmatic change, or even restructuring, is not a sufficient response to the challenges of the day. What we face is far deeper than that. We need to be talking about changing the very *culture* of mainline congregations. While much of the literature on mainline churches, their travail and prospects, is quite helpful and I draw on some of it here, my emphasis on changing the culture is, if not unique, at least distinct. So I write as a pastor and as a pastoral leader. I believe that the mainline churches will do better if we recognize our particular gifts and genius rather than trying to become someone, or something, which we are not. And yet I argue for a radical — to the roots — change and shift in the culture of mainline congregations.

The first two chapters describe the large context and great challenge we face. In the next ten chapters I trace a series of shifts and changes in congregational culture that emerged in my work and experience as critical to the challenges we face. I then conclude with a chapter on leadership, why it matters so much in this new situation, and strategies for leaders working on change in the culture of congregations. It is my hope and prayer that my contribution to the great dialogue, ferment, and redirecting of mainline Protestant congregations in North America will prove helpful to pastoral leaders, lay leaders, denominational staff and leaders — but most of all, to congregations themselves. The fact that a number of congregations and their leaders have already found this material to be helpful to them encourages me to make it available to a wider audience in this way.

I am indebted to many people, as the following chapters will make evident. I wish especially to thank Martin Copenhaver and John McFadden, colleagues in pastoral ministry whose own experience and ideas have contributed to this book. I owe a great debt of thanks to the four congregations I have been privileged to serve: Tolt Congregational

Church in Carnation, Washington; Church of the Crossroads in Honolulu, Hawaii; Shepherd of the Hills in Phoenix, Arizona; and, especially, to Plymouth Church in Seattle, Washington. Finally, I want to thank the many congregations, leadership retreats, and occasional seminary classes that have helped me to refine these concepts and sharpen them for presentation in this format.

ANTHONY B. ROBINSON

CHAPTER ONE

The Challenge We Face, Part I

I began my ordained ministry in 1977. It was the post-Watergate, post-Vietnam era. Jimmy Carter was in office. It seemed that, for better or worse, the big storms were behind us. A kind of normality appeared to have been restored. I have come to believe that in that seemingly quiet moment, large shifts and vast tremors were in fact gathering intensity at a very deep level and with quickening speed.

I had graduated from Union Theological Seminary in New York City in the spring of that year. Because I was a Northwesterner by birth, because I had gotten hooked on parish ministry while at Union (not an easy thing to do, at least at that time), and because I had developed an interest in the particular beauties, problems, and possibilities of smaller congregations, I accepted a call to a small congregation in the foothills of the Cascade Mountains, thirty-five miles east of Seattle.

Our church sat on Main Street, anchoring one end of that small logging and farming community. It was a handsome gray-granite building that looked like stability and order itself. A block away, and across the street, was the town bank. Another block west, on our side of the street, was the modest City Hall. And directly across the street from the church was the library. Kitty-corner from the church was the elementary school, and just beyond it the town cemetery. Though it was the Northwest, and not New England, it bore a certain similarity to the town greens of New England, where the institutions of civil society — the church, city hall, the school, and library — are all arrayed.

But looks are deceptive. Inside the church on Main Street a struggle was going on between traditional, civic-faith types who had dominated the church's past and still held the reins of power in the present, and a new group whose adherents identified themselves as "born-again" Christians. For the former group, the role of the church was to be one of the civic institutions gathered, if not on the town green, then on Main Street. The church was there to preserve social order, morality, and decency. The church was, as they saw it, the conscience of the community, a source of aid to the least fortunate, and a center of community and family life.

The born-again folks had a different picture. From their point of view, America was in the midst of a great spiritual crisis, one calling for repentance and conversion. The church needed to get on its battle gear and enter the fray — in the name of Jesus and against the enemies of God. The latter category, from the point of view of the born-again folks, happened to include the denomination of which we were a part! Meanwhile, in the growing suburbs east of Seattle, other changes were afoot. Reports began to circulate about new churches, rapidly growing congregations with a conservative theology, big mall-like parking lots, and a style of worship that could only be called experimental and nontraditional. What we later learned to describe as "mega-churches" were just beginning in those years.

It is ironic that it was only then, during the late seventies, that I first became aware of the term "mainline" to designate the kind of church where I was the pastor. We were the mainline church, so it was said, and in a way it was certainly true. Our congregation had been founded nearly a hundred years earlier, the first church in the town. We stood proudly on Main Street. Some of the town's leading citizens were our members, if infrequent in their attendance. And yet, if "mainline" means something like located at the center of the theological spectrum, and being at the center of the community and its life, it was less clear that we were mainline. After I had been in the area for a year or so, it struck me that the center of the theological spectrum was probably at about the Assembly of God. There were lots of little Pentecostal and Baptist churches, and assorted other fellowships and Jesus freak groups, that were considerably to the right of the Assembly of God. Our congregation, conservative or moderate by our own denomination's standards, was out on the theological left wing in that community. Moreover, we represented an aging elite, whose day of leadership in business, education, and town government had pretty much passed.

The term "mainline" was just beginning to be common usage, in other words, as churches like ours ceased to be, in any real or recognizable sense, the mainline. We were no longer at the center of the religious culture, or of the theological spectrum, or even at the center of community life. As the twenty-five years of my ministry have unfolded, it now seems clear that this shift in the religious life of our society, and its consequent change in the role of the historically mainline Protestant congregations, was a deep and building earthquake. It was in many ways not yet visible, not much perceived, in the late 1970s, the seemingly quiet era of the Carter presidency when America had been restored to order. As it has turned out, this time of seismic shift in the religious ecology of our society — the ending of one great era and the birth of a new one — has been the context in which my own ministry has unfolded and taken place. My ministry has been dominated by trying to understand these shifts and respond to them as a pastor and church leader. This book seeks to relate something of that experience and what I have learned in the course of it.

Changing American Culture

I have come to describe these sea changes in our society and in the church as changes in culture. This cuts at least two ways. Partly, I mean to say that what we are dealing with is a deep change in the culture — religious and otherwise — of North American society. An era of de facto American Christendom in which the Protestant mainline churches had been the religious establishment of the culture was ending. Furthermore, modernity and its hallmark values — reason, self-sufficiency, progress, and optimism — were losing their sense of inevitability and their taken-for-granted status. A new secular, religiously pluralistic, and postmodern culture was emerging. Secondly, I mean that a response to these shifts requires change in the culture of congregations themselves. I will return to this theme shortly, and throughout this book. But before doing so I want to consider the changes in our cultural context: in the culture of American society and in its religious ethos.

What has changed? How have the mainline Protestant churches lost their grip, such that every mainline denomination has lost churches and members continuously since 1965? Much has been written in the attempt to answer these questions. Certainly the question of mainline Protestant decline is a complex one for which there are no easy answers. Yet from where I stood, as a child of the sixties and a young pastor in the seventies, I could point to five related factors, which reflected the changes in the culture of North American society and its religious ethos that spelled trouble for mainline Protestantism.

From Obligation to Motivation

As a religious establishment, mainline churches tended to rely on a *sense of obligation* as a powerful motivator for their membership and constituency. Attending church, being part of a church, having your children baptized in the church, and sending them to Sunday school was something you were supposed to do. But if the 1960s were about anything, they were about the diminished power of social norms, accepted values and expectations, and the sense of accepted obligations. Increasingly, perhaps especially in the West, people did not simply go to or belong to a church because it was expected, because they felt an obligation to do so.

It was, as Wade Clark Roof and Bill McKinney called it, "a generation of seekers." And for this generation of seekers, *motivation replaced obligation.* If people were motivated, if they found some meaning and value in an experience for them, they would be involved. If it was only a matter of fulfilling a societal obligation, the church was losing its hold on people. Another — more theological — way to put this is to note that, in many mainline congregations, a religion of good works and achievement seemed to have supplanted a religion of grace. If being a part of a church was born of a sense of obligation, congregations themselves tended to have replaced a religion of grace with something that was much more moralistic. There were "good works" to be done. That might translate into "giving more to missions" than other churches in one's denomination; it might mean serving on many boards and committees; it might mean striving to have a "perfect family"; or it might mean having "the right values" and supporting the correct causes. The mainline ethos had, it seemed, lost the crucial and powerful element of biblical faith — grace, new life, forgiveness — and replaced it with a much more conventional morality.

Erosion of Trust and Reliable Authority

This leads to the second factor I would cite in the shifting religious ethos and the increasing difficulty of mainline churches in responding to it. Not only had motivation increasingly replaced a sense of obligation in what led people to church, but the problems people faced and sensed were deeper and darker than those that could be addressed by a civic faith that was strong on obligation and good works.

The 1960s and 70s saw a succession of events that tore holes in the sacred canopy of American society and its civil religion. There were a series of traumatic assassinations — of President Kennedy, Martin Luther King Jr., and Robert Kennedy. There was an unpopular war. There was, partly as a consequence of that war, a new drug culture. There was a political scandal, Watergate, which brought down a president. *Social trust and confidence were shattered* when the sacred canopy was torn, and authority in many forms was, if not ridiculed and rejected outright, then simply dismissed. The recent Ang Lee film *Ice Storm* does an especially good job of portraying just how much at sea parents, children, and extended families had become during the early 1970s. Lee's film shows the most successful middle-class families dying from within: parents turned to infidelity, alcohol, and drugs, and children were left floating in a world of affluence and anomie. All of this goes on in the movie against the background of President Nixon's denying any complicity in Watergate — lying to the American people. The divorce rate was rising toward fifty percent; legalized abortion became for many another form of birth control; people felt less safe as drug use, crime, and violence became endemic; and once-reliable authority figures — from presidents to pastors — seemed to be missing in action.

The problems were deep — deeper than those that could be addressed or touched by a civic faith that had been persuasive and even powerful in an era when the sacred canopy was whole, when social norms had greater power, and when institutions and authority figures were trusted and respected.

Social trust had broken down, and reliable authority had been lost. Increasingly, people came to church, if they did so at all, seeking something like healing, salvation, and hope for themselves and their families. One could no longer assume the kind of familial stability and strength of individual character that allowed so many mainline congregations to call strong and gifted people to service. Those who were once comfortable and stable were now among the afflicted.

New Religious Pluralism

A third factor was the way that America, as a consequence of the Immigration and Naturalization Act of 1965, rapidly became a much more *ethnically and religiously diverse society.* Up until that time, American immigration quotas reflected the racism of American society itself. But as the civil rights movement brought an end to legally sanctioned segregation, the Immigration and Naturalization Act of 1965 opened up the United States to a new wave of immigrants who were much more diverse than had been true in the past. However one evaluates these changes (they were good and just in my view), they have ended up having a steady but enormous impact over several decades. In the small town in western Washington where I began my ministry there was virtually no ethnic or cultural diversity in 1977. All the citizens were of European descent: some were Scandinavian, others Swiss, many English and Irish, some Eastern European. That all began to change in 1978, when Southeast Asian refugees arrived in increasing numbers. Our congregation sponsored Hmong families from Laos, people who were casualties of the Vietnam War in that they had been allied with the Americans and now were at risk in Vietnam, Laos, and Cambodia. By the time our family left that small town three years later (1981), 10 percent of its population of 700 were Hmong.

With regional variations, this was happening all over America during the late 1960s, 70s, and 80s. Some of these new immigrants, such as the Hmong, brought with them religious traditions of animism; others brought the Islamic faith; still others brought Hinduism and Buddhism. For the first time, numbers of Americans confronted religions other than Judaism and Christianity down the street or next door to them rather than around the other side of the globe. For the first time, Americans confronted ethnic and racial diversity that went beyond the familiar, if still problematic, black and white.

As the twenty-first century begins, we are merely beginning to come to grips with these changes and how enormous they have been. In many metropolitan school districts, for instance, students now come from between fifty and seventy different language groups. There are now more Muslims in the United States than Presbyterians. More than fifty percent of the population of California is made up of people of color. For some these changes are welcome; for others they are threatening. But for all Americans — and for American society as a whole — they are significant. In a compressed time, the American population has gone from predominantly European-American to being much more racially and ethnically diverse. During that same period, the country has gone from a religiously homogeneous Christian culture to a religiously pluralistic society.

If mainline Protestant congregations did a good job, by and large, of welcoming the newcomers and making a home for them in America, these same congregations were less successful in helping their own members do what any pluralistic situation requires: giving a credible account of one's own faith and one's reasons for holding it. Inevitably, the presence of "the Other" raises questions about who we are and what that means. The fact that one's neighbors now were Muslims, Buddhists, or Hindus inevitably raised questions for American Christians: What do we believe? How are we to express our faith? What are our particular religious practices and spiritual disciplines? Civic religion was, by and large, not well prepared to help its constituencies answer these questions.

While serving a congregation in Hawaii, where the largest religious group in the population is Buddhist, I participated in "interfaith dialogues" between the Buddhist and Christian communities. Generally, it was mainline Protestants who were open to and interested in that dialogue. Fundamentalist and evangelical Protestants were not interested. But the dialogue ran into a difficulty: the mainline Protestants' theology was often so thin that there was not much to dialogue about. Certainly this was an irony: the "open" Christians were so open that they didn't have much to say! But it also suggested the problem facing the mainline in a new era of religious pluralism in a postmodern time. Suddenly, the moralistic sentiments of civic religion were not enough. Buddhists and

Muslims — not to mention secularists — could be decent, caring people and good citizens. Civic religion had not prepared mainline Protestants to be able to give an account of their faith to their new neighbors or even — and this was perhaps more serious — to their children.

Another way to put this is to say that the erosion of social trust and reliable authority, coupled with a new religious and cultural diversity and pluralism, had thrust a new generation into postmodern society. There was no longer a binding story or narrative that made sense of human life for most everyone. And there was an increasing suspicion of such metanarratives, of any attempt to say that all human beings or all human experience could be understood by means of any one explanatory or interpretive perspective. Increasingly, North American culture was many cultures, many stories, many perspectives, and many centers.

Even more perhaps than the "baby-boomers" (those born between 1946 and 1964), were the so-called "Gen X'ers (born after 1964) part of the emerging postmodern society. But the generation that was still in charge in the mainline churches — partly because the baby-boomers had exited those churches in vast numbers — was the pre–World War II generation, the generation of modernity. For that generation there was still a binding story — that is, the American civil religion — and there was still a sense of norms that applied across the board. These assumptions of modernity, which included a trust in reason, progress, technology, and tolerance (the benchmark values of modernity), lost traction in the emerging postmodern society. Postmoderns notably lacked confidence in the American story, in civil religion, in progress, and in reason or technology. Theirs was a more fragmented, decentered world of rapid shifts, disposable identities, and changing images — the world, as some have said, of MTV.

Mainline Protestantism and Modernity

If amid the new religious and cultural diversity of North America, and the erosion of social trust and once reliable authority, a new postmodern culture was emerging, this spelled particular trouble for churches that had hooked their star, so to speak, to modernity and its theological project, liberalism. But that is exactly what the mainline Protestant churches had done. As the religious establishment of North

America, we had embraced the dominant values of modernity so fully that, as the ethos of modernity came under increasing questioning and lost its sense of inevitability, the mainline congregations and denominations lacked the capacity to critically assess modernity and its values.

Some of the most characteristic values of modernity, as noted earlier, have been the reliance on reason, the emphasis on individual and human self-sufficiency, and a great sense of optimism, a belief in progress. While voices within mainline Protestantism, such as Reinhold Niebuhr, did critically assess these values and their congruence with the historic claims of Christian faith, theirs were minority voices that never really seemed to gain an enduring foothold in the churches. Instead, congregations and their leaders were often unable or unwilling to maintain any real element of Christian distinctiveness or a capacity to challenge regnant cultural values. Thus, while increasing numbers of people were becoming disillusioned with modernity's claims and values and might have turned to the Christian faith as an alternative, mainline Protestantism did not offer much of an alternative. Instead, we sounded pretty much like the dominant culture, where a commitment to reason, individual autonomy, progress, and optimism held sway.

During the 1960s and 70s, one might hear a left-of-center political critique in mainline congregations, but even that remained within the dominant paradigm of modernity. Such critiques tended to assume that the world was in our hands and that with sufficient resolve on our part and enough letters to our congressmen things would get straightened out. There was little capacity to speak of the intrusive and often disturbing grace of God, or of the God for whom all things are possible and who brings life out of death. This was just too odd for churches that had come to depend on their established status.

Moreover, liberalism, the theological and philosophical project that undergirded mainline churches, had as its primary goal making Christian faith intelligible and acceptable to modernity. (In speaking of "liberalism" here, I am speaking of theology and philosophy, not politics.) If fundamentalism, theologically, represented a circle-the-wagons reaction against modernity, theological liberalism was the opposite: it was the attempt to make the Christian faith and gospel "fit" the modern world, to show that it was really reasonable and that it supported individualism, self-sufficiency, optimism, and progress. Theological liberalism adjusted the Christian faith to modernity, but at a price: the defining and distinctive characteristics of the Christian faith were eroded, diminished, and, in time, forgotten. The ability of the churches informed by theological liberalism to critique the culture of modernity was seriously hampered, if not altogether lost.

The Complacency of an Establishment

A fifth factor in the changing religious ethos of North American society, and a reason mainline Protestant congregations were losing their hold and connection in that culture, was something that always bedevils established groups — complacency. Too often mainline congregations and leaders assumed that they had a guaranteed place and constituency. And why not? After all, we stood on the main streets, at the center of downtowns, and on the town greens of America. As obligation was replaced by motivation, as social trust and reliable authority broke down, as a new wave of immigration brought religious diversity, the Protestant mainline was slow to recognize its own jeopardy. It tended to assume its place, relevance, importance, and constituency would always exist.

This was evident in a number of specific ways to which mainline Protestants have now, belatedly, awoken. One was complacency about leadership. Mainline Protestants had ceased to have any real system for recruiting promising clergy. Gradually, already beginning in the 1970s, the age of seminarians rose to the point that fewer and fewer were giving a lifetime to ministry, and more and more were coming to it as a second career. Often the 40- and 50-year-olds now going through seminary and entering ministry brought important life experience; but they also often came from situations where they had not experienced success or accomplishment. No longer did congregations, whose membership was growing markedly older, have a pool of youth to encourage toward ministry. No longer did the best and the brightest make the move from college to seminary. And those who did go to seminary often found schools that had not begun to recognize the changes in the landscape of religious America; these seminaries were still training leaders for the Protestant establishment.

Mainline Protestantism had a leadership problem in part because a whole network of church-related liberal arts colleges across the country had loosened their own ties to the churches that once sponsored and supported them. This may have been unavoidable; but its impact has been great. Hundreds of such colleges were once part of the ethos of the Protestant mainline, providing a flow of men and women not only toward ordained ministry but toward lay leadership in the churches as well. In the 1960s and 70s, many of these colleges either severed the historic ties to their churches altogether or rendered those ties so nominal as to be invisible. Often the ties were loosened with the best of intentions, that is, to embrace religious pluralism and diversity. But the upshot was that mainline Protestantism lost a critical component of its own culture, a training ground for its own leaders and constituency.

Besides the leadership problems, and the loss of the colleges, the mainline denominations had themselves become bureaucratized: large, complex structures and national organizations were often distant from the grassroots. These elaborate organizations may have been suited to the now passing era of American Christendom, but as their constituent congregations faced the changes in American culture and its religious ethos, they were not well suited to respond. What they were well suited to do was to carry on an existing, established church; they were not ready or able to lead, or in many cases, even to perceive change. Instead of finding in their denominational offices and structures a ready resource and support, many church leaders and congregations found these same structures a burden, something else to support in increasingly difficult times of diminished resources. Businesses such as IBM may have seen the handwriting on the wall and moved rapidly to streamline and reorganize; but mainline denominations, by and large, did not begin streamlining and reorganizing until it was too late — with too little. Denominational restructuring efforts have been more a bowing to necessity than restructuring for a new kind of church and mission.

Others have pointed to other factors in the cultural change: demographic shifts from the east to the west, declining birth rates among the mainline, and a shifting financial base, among others. But these five — from obligation to motivation, the breakdown of social trust and reliable authority, new immigration and religious pluralism, the Protestant mainline's stifling embrace of modernity, and simple complacency on the part of the Protestant mainline — seem to me to be the most salient shifts in American culture and its religious ethos that have spelled decline for the mainline Protestant churches.

CHAPTER TWO

The Challenge We Face, Part II

Changing the Culture of Congregations

If part of what we are dealing with is change in the larger North American culture and society — its religious makeup and ethos, I will also use "culture" and "cultural change" in a second sense. Response to these larger cultural shifts on the part of the once mainline churches will involve change in the culture of congregations. Programmatic change is not enough. Restructuring is not enough. Neither will go deep enough. Most clergy and church leaders get half a dozen mailings each week that describe the latest, hottest, and newest program for congregational renewal. Some of them are quite good. But few of them get to the level of change in the *culture* of the congregation. (Here I am using the term "culture" in an anthropological sense to mean the thick network of symbols, language, and behaviors that characterize and define a human community.) The challenge we face in the historically mainline Protestant churches is the challenge of cultural change in this latter sense.

As I have written and spoken to groups on this challenge, I have found helpful a basic distinction made by Ronald Heifetz in his book *Leadership Without Easy Answers.* Heifetz distinguishes between "technical work" and "adaptive challenge." Technical work is characterized by being able to clearly define a problem and clearly define the solution. For example, the church school classrooms are too crowded; the problem is clear and so is the solution: add space, build a new wing to the education building. Adaptive work, on the other hand, is not so clear. The problem may in some cases be known, but the solution requires learning and change. An instructive analogy might be heart disease. The doctors can diagnose heart disease; the problem can be clearly named; but there are a variety of possible solutions. Moreover, all of the solutions will require that the patient do some learning, about himself and the illness. Furthermore, effective response will require life changes: a different diet, a new regimen of exercise, different work habits, and general stress reduction. All of that adds up to deep change in a person's life.

An analogy in the life of congregations might be a change in the community that surrounds a congregation and from which it draws its members. Perhaps the community goes from predominantly Caucasian to Asian or Hispanic. The challenge or shift can be clearly named: change in the ethnic makeup of the community. But how to respond to that change turns out to be no simple matter of putting up an "Everyone Welcome" sign — even if it's in Spanish and Tagalog. Learning is required. Change in the internal life, self-perceptions, and culture of the congregation will be necessary if it is to respond to these shifts in the community.

Here is another set of analogies, this time drawn from my own life. Over the years I have found that I am susceptible to sinus and ear infections. Especially when I fly there is a probability that I will develop one of these irritating maladies. But they have happened often enough that I have gotten pretty good at diagnosing them. The problem is known and can be clearly described, either by me or by a doctor. What's more, the solution is also clear: take this antibiotic for seven to ten days, and it should clear up. But twenty-some years ago I encountered a wholly different kind of problem. I had no notion what was going on. All I knew was that I felt hollowed out from the inside. Life had lost its pleasure, hope, and meaning. I went home after church one day and lay down on the bed, unsure whether I would, or could, get up again. As it happened, I did get up again and continued on doggedly with my work and life — but savoring none of it. I felt as though I were dead or dying inside.

In time, I was able to give a name to what I was experiencing: I called it "depression." I might just as well — and perhaps more usefully — have named it "a dark night of the soul," for it certainly was that. But my point here is that, in contrast to my experience with sinus infections, I was unable to clearly name the problem. Even to name the problem required learning and change. It required learning to say that something was wrong and that I needed help. Both were new, different, and difficult experiences for me. Once I was able to name what I was experiencing, there was still huge learning and change involved in the solution. Medication helped, but other steps were required. I had to do some rethinking of ministry and of the ways I had learned to do it. I had to learn — in a way that I had managed not to thus far — to trust in and rely on God and the Holy Spirit. I had to learn not only to preach grace but also to allow myself to receive and experience grace. I had to become less attached to outcomes and more open to letting God be God.

That dark night of the soul was a profound adaptive challenge for me. Neither the problem nor the solution had easy answers; they required learning and change. They also had something to do with the deep changes, the cultural shifts, looming for mainline churches. I had had a sense of those shifts but had no language to name them, much less begin to respond to them. That created a good deal of internal, spiritual struggle for me. I had been prepared by background and education to be a pastor for a church and world that were vanishing. So at the same time that I was wandering in my wilderness, finding manna and water in surprising places, I was part of a similar wilderness journey in the churches I knew and loved. We too were facing an adaptive challenge, but for the most part we were unable to see it as such. Instead, we thought we had a technical problem on our hands.

In virtually all of the mainline Protestant denominations, we named our problem as "membership decline." There was no question that membership was declining. Since the mid-1960s, my denomination's individual membership, as well as its number of congregations, had been in steady decline. And this was basically true of every mainline Protestant denomination in North America. So during the 1980s most of those denominations identified the problem as "membership decline." On the local church level, the solution was to be "membership growth techniques and strategies"; on the denominational level, the solution was membership growth combined with relocation of the denominational headquarters to be closer to the grassroots — plus denominational restructuring. Thus, in the local churches we dutifully went off to "evangelism workshops" and training in church-growth techniques. We had named the problem and the solution. Both were clear. All we needed to do was take our antibiotics — our membership growth techniques: wear nametags, improve the signage, greet visitors in a warm and friendly (but not too friendly) way, and get a gung-ho attitude toward growth.

But it didn't work. It didn't work because we had mistaken a technical problem for an adaptive challenge. We had thought we could deal with this at a programmatic level. More "New Member Sundays," better hospitality, and superior usher training. None of this was bad to do, and some of it was quite good. But our problems were much deeper and more challenging. They involved changes in the culture of the congregation and of the denomination. They involved a new kind of learning, and there were no easy answers. In fact, we didn't really even know how to define the problem we were dealing with. Just to begin to understand it and name it would involve learning and change in perception. We were not facing a technical problem; we were facing an adaptive challenge.

Our Adaptive Challenge

As I began to name the adaptive challenge for myself and for others, my names for it represented not conclusive or fully adequate descriptions but something more like hunches, hints, and guesses. One way to put the adaptive challenge we face is to say that we are no longer living in the world of American Christendom. Many of those in leadership in mainline congregations, including me, had grown up in that world of American Christendom, a world where Christianity was the unofficial official religion of our society. The church and culture were interwoven in ways that we were mostly unaware of — because we were accustomed to them. For example, in the East during the 1950s (I was born in Oregon but grew up in a suburb of Washington, D.C.), all the stores were closed on Sunday. That just seemed normal; but it was, in fact, a central way in which the church was supported by the culture. Not only were stores closed on Sundays, but not much of anything else happened on Sundays either — except church. No youth sports, no charity walks or runs, no college sports. All of this was part of American Christendom.

There were other aspects to the subtle interweaving of church and society. My school day typically began with the Pledge of Allegiance to the American flag; but often there was also a prayer and sometimes a reading from the Bible. During the holidays there were Christmas pageants at the public school and in the community, complete with the singing of Christian carols and songs. Whenever there was a civic event, a local Christian clergyman would begin the affair with an invocation and end it with a benediction. In all these ways, Christianity was the established religion of the society, and it was with these customs that most previous generations of Americans had grown up. There were regional exceptions and variations, but this was enough the norm that we can speak of American Christendom.

Moreover, it was the mainline Protestant churches that were the religious establishment of this culture. The Congregationalists, Methodists, Presbyterians, Baptists, some Lutherans, and Episcopalians stood proudly on town greens, main streets, and in downtowns as the center of religion and culture. The Assemblies of God, various Pentecostal groups, and other "off-brand" Protestants did exist, but they were on the sidelines. In the 1950s, even the Roman Catholics were still on the sidelines, perceived as an immigrant church.

But in the 1960s and 70s, the mainline Protestant denominations were disestablished — sometimes by legal means, such as the outlawing of prayer in public schools, but more often by shifts in the culture and its ethos. American culture was on its way to becoming an officially secular, religiously pluralistic, and racially and ethnically heterogeneous society. I am not suggesting that this was a direction to be lamented; it was simply different, very different. For congregations that were used to being at the center of the culture, even the religious center of the culture, the mainline, it was a change so great that we could hardly even perceive it.

We in the mainline churches found ourselves dealing with some of the things that characterize an adaptive challenge. Our deeply held beliefs were being challenged. For example, to Christendom and civic faith types, everyone in our society was sort of a Christian, or so we thought. But then people began to differentiate, to speak of "becoming Christian" in the way one might speak of becoming Buddhist. This was different and odd, not something we were accustomed to or prepared to deal with. We had forgotten how to do basic Christian formation. Everyone who grew up in America was already a sort of Christian, weren't they?

Not only were our deeply held beliefs challenged; the values and strategies that had served us well in the Christendom era no longer worked so well either. We noticed, for example, that people popped in to have their baby "done," or baptized, but they didn't stay. We seldom saw them again, unless it was on the soccer field. Once such an understanding of baptism — as joining the church, society, and community — had worked pretty well. But increasingly it made less sense, and it certainly no longer guaranteed that a family would become regulars at church or that the child would march on through Sunday school toward confirmation.

Finally, there were a host of legitimate, competing alternatives looming on the horizon. Some were secular: "Oh, we have family things on Sundays. We go skiing. It's our one day to rest and get the things done we need to do for Monday." But others of the new alternatives were religious, as people were drawn to different kinds of churches and religious experiences. Some went to the new nondenominational megachurches. Others drifted into different kinds of spiritual journeys — Eastern spiritual practices and New Age groups that offered an amalgam of spirituality and self-help. Suddenly there were a host of alternatives for the spiritually seeking, a whole new menu of possibilities from which to choose. Fewer people were showing up in the once established churches out of a sense of obligation, a sense that it was simply what one did as a good citizen and decent person.

Another way to describe our huge adaptive challenge is to say that the modern era is over. Some weird new thing, awkwardly dubbed "postmodernity," has been emerging. The modern era, in which Americans had a unifying story and a shared confidence in self-sufficiency, reason, science, technology, progress, and optimism, has been on the wane. In the 1950s and 60s, for example, there had been three major networks on television, and in most respects there wasn't much difference between the three: what constituted news for all three was pretty much the same. There was a shared story, one unifying narrative. But by the 1980s, cable had come and satellite disks were popping up on and around homes like mushrooms. Instead of three networks with one overriding sense of reality and a dominant social story, suddenly there were fifty stations — or if you wanted to buy the technology, a hundred or more. There was no single narrative any longer. Reality was a plurality of narratives, from many different perspectives. People were considerably less sure than they had once been what it meant to be an American, a citizen, even to be a man or a woman. The notion of "common human experience" began to be less common, less agreed on. People began to doubt that there is a "world" — self-evident, natural, normal — just sitting out there. Everybody, we realized, lives somewhere. Everybody is standing somewhere. Modernity lingered, but it no longer had the grip it once had. Because mainline Protestant congregations had hooked their wagon to the star of modernity, they were less able to perceive and respond to this new situation.

So it was not a technical problem that the churches faced. "Membership decline," while real, did not begin to adequately name our situation. It was, and is, an enormous adaptive challenge posed by a newly post-Christendom, post-establishment, postmodern era. Different congregations would experience the challenge differently depending on their setting, their denomination, and their particular history. But for all the mainline Protestant denominations that had once been the religious establishment of a more or less Christian America, where there was a high degree of consensus and homogeneity, the challenge was enormous and painful. It felt like loss, and in many ways it was. There was loss of numbers, loss of clout, loss of role, loss of certainty. All this loss, and its attendant grief, has spawned an era of conflict and uncertainty in mainline congregations and denominations. What has been less clear is that these shifts also hold wonderful opportunities and rich possibilities. Understandably, these have been harder to see. Congregations have been stung by never-ending conflict. Clergy have lost their way and have often been the scapegoats. Denominations and their leaders have also been the scapegoats and, despite attempts to get closer to the grassroots by relocating headquarters and restructuring, have found themselves distrusted and distanced.

But I honestly believe that these are birth pangs, not death throes. Or, if they are death throes, they can be experienced with a certain hopefulness, because for Christians, death precedes a resurrection. Walter Brueggemann captured it when he told a gathering of mainline clergy: "The world for which you have been so carefully preparing is being taken away from you, by the grace of God."

There are signs of new life among us as the new century emerges. They are not uniform, and they are not conclusive; we are very much still trying to figure out what they are. But there are, it is clear, possibilities of new life. Moreover, there are opportunities for being the church in authentic and deep ways that may not have been possible in our establishment era.

Leadership in Culture Change

To see and respond to these opportunities requires a great deal of leaders, whether clergy or lay leaders. It is not an easy time to be in leadership in the mainline Protestant denominations or congregations. But — paradoxically perhaps — it is a very good time to be in leadership. It is a good time, in part, because leading people in the face of — and to face — adaptive challenges draws on our best and deepest spiritual resources. Adaptive challenges are, at their core, spiritual work. They ask of us learning, authenticity, depth, risk, and change. They ask of us precisely the kind of work that Scripture prepares us to do. Adaptive challenge requires the kind of spiritual practices and discipline that our different traditions offer and teach.

It is a good time to be the church and a good time to be a leader in the church, provided we recognize the enormous adaptive challenges that come with the dying of one era and the birth of a new one. It is a good time to be a leader in the church, provided we recognize that leadership in the midst of adaptive challenge is a different kind of leadership from the leadership required in more stable periods and institutions. In his work, Heifetz notes five characteristic roles and functions of leaders: *direction, protection, orientation, dealing with conflict,* and *establishing norms.* While these roles and functions of leaders continue whether one is dealing with adaptive challenge or not, the way leaders go about them changes radically.

In more stable times, or when one is dealing with routine or technical problems, leaders typically provide direction by giving answers and furnishing solutions. So, for example, the identified problem of a given congregation may be: "we need to strengthen our financial resources, or have better stewardship." While the long-term answer involves adaptive change, congregations can and will expect that their leaders have some notions about how to help people think about stewardship, how to put together an effective drive, and encourage significant giving. In other words, in facing a technical problem, a leader provides answers.

But today, and in the midst of adaptive challenges, leadership requires more than providing solutions to technical problems. It also requires a quite different, and more challenging, skill: asking questions. Sometimes the questions that need to be asked are quite simple. But while the questions may be simple or basic, the answers are not. For example, when I interviewed with the search committee of the congregation I presently serve, I asked, "What are you, as a congregation, trying to accomplish?" That is an important question for churches facing adaptive challenge. Why are we here, and what are we trying to do? But it turns out that this is not an easy question for the long-established church to answer. Generally what has happened in long-established congregations is that mission and purpose have gotten lost or become confused with maintaining the church as an organization. Maintaining and surviving — and keeping the membership satisfied — have tended to become what we are trying to accomplish, even if we are unaware of it, even if we pay lip service to other goals and values. Any other, or any very clear, sense of mission or purpose has been eclipsed. That this is the case is all the more reason for those who would offer leadership in the face of adaptive challenge to ask questions as they seek to give direction to the life of a congregation.

Protection is another characteristic function of leaders. The role of a leader is often to protect the body or group from external threat. So, for example, noting the new and growing mega-church five miles away, a pastor might point out the ways in which the new church is seemingly selling a product rather than proclaiming the gospel. "Look at the way their services are entertainment," such a pastor might say, not the real thing, which by implication is what "we" offer. Such would be a way of protecting the congregation and its members from the alternative and threat posed by new religious expression.

Leaders in the midst of adaptive change may offer a thoughtful critique of different options, whether they be mega-church or New Age spirituality, but they will do something else as well: they will allow their congregations to feel what Heifetz terms "the pinch of reality." "You may have noticed, friends, that many of your children have been attracted to alternative spiritual paths, while your grandchildren are going to conservative mega-churches. I wonder how you feel about that? I wonder what it might be saying to us?" In this way the leader may let the group feel the pinch of reality rather than protecting the congregation from it by ignoring such new realities or simply judging them. Without some pressure, some pinch of reality, adaptive work is unlikely to happen. If people, to put it another way, are too comfortable, nothing will change.

A third function of leaders that is of a more technical or routine nature is to orient people to their roles and to the expectations of the group and its culture. This is a good part of what goes on in a typical "new members' class" or "inquirers' class." What is expected of a member of this congregation? How do I become a member? What do I need to know about this tribe of Christians and their ways of doing and being?

But sometimes, when facing adaptive change, it is the role of the leader not only to orient but to disorient people, to challenge the accustomed roles and expectations, and to dislodge people from their well-known roles. In one congregation I served there were five worship services; but this was not because the church was overflowing with people. It was because the strategy for holding onto the membership was to create a lot of different kinds of services to suit different sensibilities. There was a service for those who liked organ music, another for guitar types, a third for early risers who didn't need a choir, a fourth for those who didn't like music at all, another for people who like to have their kids with them and sing children's ditties. Everyone was safely tucked in his or her own preferred box, and worship was as dull as dishwater. I undertook to disorient people by suggesting that we mix it all up on "Festival Sundays" — all ages, all kinds of music and instruments, different arts, and worship with people who were not in your particular group. Needless to say, for some this was disorienting and deeply disturbing; but for many others it was an experience of richness in which they found new life.

A fourth role of leaders is to deal with conflict in the group or body. Many leaders in mainline churches have somehow gotten the idea that the worst thing that can happen in a church is conflict. A good church is one where everyone gets along, everything goes smoothly, and no one is ever upset. It just so happens that, if you ever find a church where this is true all the time, chances are very good that lots of stuff is being swept under the rug, and the illusion of harmony is just that. Human groups, even churches — perhaps especially churches — have conflict.

In the midst of adaptive change, leaders will not simply manage or quell conflict, they will draw it out. To be sure, they will do so thoughtfully, trying to discern which conflicts are substantive and which are not. They will not unleash too many conflicts at any one time because people simply can't deal with an overload in a way that will be constructive rather than destructive. But the point is that, in the midst of adaptive change, conflict can be a way to do important learning and changing. Getting a particular conflict out on the table can help people air important issues. Rather than panicking at the first sign of conflict, an effective leader will help people take it out, look at it, and see it for what it's worth. When things are too placid, good leaders will stir things up, start some trouble.

Leaders not only provide direction, protection, orientation, and deal with conflict, they also interpret and establish group norms. "This has been our style and history, what we have found to be effective, or the way we have gone about this," are the kinds of things leaders say as they reinforce the norms of a particular group or congregation. But in times of adaptive change, leaders will do something else as well. At least on occasion, they will question the norms, the status quo, the "way we've always done it." Why do we always have the children go out of the service before the sermon? What are we saying when we do that? Whose interests are being served by this strategy? Why do we send our mission dollars to the regional and national offices of the denomination? Why is that our mission? What does that say about how we understand mission?

To be sure, asking questions is not easy and will seldom be well received. In many respects what I have described as giving leadership for facing adaptive challenge — asking questions, letting people feel the pinch of reality, dis-orienting, drawing out conflict, challenging norms — is the work of a prophet. And we all know what happens to prophets! The kinds of things leaders do in more stable situations, and in more technical roles — provide answers, protect, orient, quell conflict, and reinforce group norms — might be thought of as a more priestly style of leadership. In reality, congregations need both, and clergy and lay leaders in congregations need to provide both. Yet in our day the pastor may need to lean more toward the prophetic role, especially since there are such powerful forces in the church and culture pushing pastors toward more socially congenial roles of peacemaker, reconciler, smoother of ruffled feathers, and but another of the helping professions — trying to make life a little easier, a little less stressful.

The Leader's Allies

In this prophetic role, in the task of asking questions, challenging norms, and exposing conflict, the pastor does have some significant allies: Jesus and the Bible, to name two. So far as I can tell, Jesus was not mainly in the business of providing answers, managing and quelling conflict, or reinforcing communal norms. Rather, he drew attention to the gap between present realities and the Kingdom, which is another way of describing an adaptive challenge: it is where there is a gap, a dissonance between the values and ideals we profess and the realities we live. Scripture, too, is more of an ally in this adaptive work than many suspect. Scripture is not a book of moral examples, a sort of really old book of virtues. No, Scripture tells the story of God's intrusions into our settled worlds, of God's determination to turn over the world as it is and to form a people for God's glory. This God is not in the business of keeping things tidy, nailed down, and predictable. Rather this is a God who disturbs the status quo, breaks open the settled worlds, reverses the world's order, and raises the dead. So the pastor and preacher who takes seriously the work of leadership of this sort will find in our Lord and in the Scriptures and stories of our faith wonderful allies.

Too often we preachers have taken it as our task to make the faith fit in with the modern world rather than to challenge it. We have exercised technical leadership, but not leadership for adaptive change. So, for example, in the early years of my ministry I was often confronted by people who said, "You know I have trouble with Easter, the Resurrection. Just can't buy it." Translation: "I am a modern, scientific, enlightened person." I would try to make it easier for them by saying: "Well, it's a symbol, a metaphor, about our various dyings and risings." Over the years I have come to believe that I am more faithful — and probably ultimately more helpful — as a pastor when I let the trouble stand, when I don't try to smooth it all out and make it easy.

So now when someone says, "I have trouble with Easter — because I'm a modern person and I just can't buy it," I say: "Well, yes, that's not surprising, you live in a closed world, a world that is fully explained and predictable. No wonder you have trouble with Easter, with the claim that God is breaking into the world, doing a new thing, that God can raise the dead. This is difficult for satisfied moderns. But take heart, with God all things are possible."

As mainline Protestant bodies face the adaptive challenges posed by a post-Christendom era, by our disestablished status, and by postmodernity, leaders will need to find the ways and the courage to be prophetic in these particular ways. To bring about change in the culture of congregations will require just such loving, gutsy, bold leadership. Never to challenge, question, disorient, or lead people onto the risky terrain of conflict can hardly be called leadership. It may be a fine institutional chaplaincy, but it is not pastoral leadership. In reality, that is avoiding leadership rather than exercising it. It tends to shut out, or quench, the Holy Spirit rather than inviting or permitting it. It more effectively keeps people dependent than it helps them to grow into a mature Christian faith and life.

If you are in the market for an adventure, it is a great time to be a leader in the church. And because the church today is facing such an important and essential challenge, it is a wondrously exciting time for ministries that help congregations enter into cultural change and the new life that comes with it.

CHAPTER THREE

From Civic Faith to Human Transformation

Asking Questions: Purpose

In the midst of adaptive challenge, it is the work of leaders, whether lay or clergy, to ask questions. Sometimes the best questions are the most basic ones, the seemingly simple ones. I have a journalist friend who likes to preface his most incisive questions with the coy introduction, "This is probably a stupid question, but . . ." It often turns out that the simplest, most basic, even "stupid" question is the one others have been afraid to ask.

Peter Drucker, famed teacher of management and consultant to many of America's corporations, has made a career out of asking two such simple questions: "What business are you in?" and "How's business?" Some in the church may take exception to the use of the word "business" in the ecclesiastical context, but it is simply another word for "purpose" or "mission." Thus the Drucker questions might be rephrased: "What is your purpose?" and "How's it going?"

In the era of American Christendom, when Christianity was the unofficial official religion of North America, and when a half dozen mainline Protestant denominations were the religious establishment of the country, the business of the church might have been described by the phrase "civic faith." The job of the churches seemed to be to provide a kind of religious ethos for American culture and society. Supported by the culture, the churches returned the favor by playing a useful role in the society.

Civic Faith: The Conscience of the Community

As the purpose of the church, civic faith — providing a religious ethos for the society — can be broken down into several components. For one, the church was to be the "conscience of the community." It was a kind of prophet Nathan in his role before King David. The church was to articulate the moral claims and requirements, to be the voice of conscience on the issues of the day. By and large, the churches did a good job of that as they often stood in the forefront of change and calling the culture to accountability. It is not that being the conscience of the community was wrong: but in our new time it no longer fits the way it once did. For one thing, in a secular and religiously pluralistic society, no one group or even one religion can lay claim to being *the* exclusive voice of conscience in the community. There are many voices and perspectives today (even within the Christian community); the churches can — and should — be one of the voices at the table, but we are no longer the table's host, nor is it *our* table. Our culture is a postmodern one in which no one big narrative or perspective holds sway or is deferred to by all the others.

Moreover, it is increasingly true in our North American culture — especially so in the Pacific Northwest, where I live — that the church and Christianity can claim no special entrée or privilege to speak or to be heard by the culture at large. In fact, something like the opposite may be true: many settings are suspicious or dismissive of those who would speak as Christians. There is a further problem with the civic faith role and purpose of the church as the conscience of the community, a dimension of the problem that is more internal to the church itself. The church's self-understanding as the conscience of the community tended to distort the gospel itself and tilt the church toward moralistic interpretations of the Christian faith. One could get the impression growing up in the heyday of civic faith that it was the church's job to be a kind of moral policeman for the culture. Indeed, the word "Christian" was often primarily defined in moral terms. A "Christian," or "a good Christian," was a morally exemplary person rather than someone whose life was defined and shaped by a particular theological perspective.

A decade before I arrived in that small town in the foothills of the Cascade Mountains to serve my first congregation, the community had held a contest to identify the town's "best Christian," and the award had gone to the town's only Jew, the owner of the local dry goods store. Mr. Miller *was* an extremely kind and friendly man: he never said a bad word about anyone, and he was always there to help out in the community. He knew everyone and everyone knew him. Still, it must have been odd for him to receive the "best Christian in town" award! Moreover, the irony points out how "Christian" had come to be defined by qualities such as "nice," "friendly," "helpful," and "a good member of the community" — rather than any defining theology or related faith practices.

Not only did this moralizing of the Christian faith turn the church into a fellowship of the lawful and righteous (or at least "the nice") rather than a fellowship of the forgiven; it tended to distort the gospel itself. It turned the gospel into primarily an imperative. In that scheme, to be a Christian meant, first of all, a certain set of moral behaviors and attitudes. But it got the gospel backwards. The gospel, as Harry Emerson Fosdick pointed out, is first indicative before it is imperative. The indicative of the gospel concerns grace: it is about what God has done and is doing. Only after hearing the indicative of grace and then having it take root do we move to the gospel's imperative. Another way to put this is to say that the gospel message is not "Be good and then God will love you"; the gospel message is "You are loved — so be who you are, a beloved child of God." Ours is not a religion of virtue, as civic faith tended to make it, but a religion of grace.

In the civic faith era, many seemed to come to the conclusion that God's first word was the Ten Commandments. Post them on the wall of schoolrooms and courthouses! In fact, however, the Ten Commandments were not God's first word but God's second word. The first word was God's act of grace and liberation in the Exodus. The Ten Commandments described the way of life God intended for those who had been redeemed, who had known God's saving love and action. When torn from this larger context, as civic faith often did, Christianity became moralistic and legalistic. Of course, this was not always the case. At times the conscience of the community role was rooted in a profound understanding of God's grace. But the point is that today the church — and especially the mainline Protestant churches — is one voice among many without a lock or monopoly on moral credibility in the wider society.

A further problem with the role of the mainline churches as "conscience of the community" is that their witness tended to lose a distinctive or particularly Christian quality and vision. Often in the effort to speak to the community as a whole, a community whose understanding of Christian faith and theology may have been superficial, the witness of the church came to sound like conventional wisdom; the particular ways in which the gospel challenges conventional wisdom were diminished and lost. As the church sought to be the conscience of the community, the truth of the gospel ceased to be strange, and the proclamation of the church became more like the editorial pages of the morning newspaper, the reflections of secular magazines, and the enlightened observations of politicians and philosophers.

The inevitable difficulty for any faith that becomes the established faith and religion is that its sharp edges are smoothed, its distinctive qualities are blunted, and the church ceases to be a place where the word is fresh and alive. People began to ask, "Do I need to go church to hear this?"

Instrument of Aid

A second common component of civic faith was for the church to be the primary instrument of aid and assistance to the least fortunate in the society. In many ways, the church was a kind of conduit: it received the resources (tangible and monetary) of the most fortunate and directed them toward those in need. Again, my point is not that there was something wrong with this. There is not. The church should continue to be a shelter for the shelterless, a harbor for the harborless, giving food to the hungry, drink to the thirsty. But just as the church is no longer the exclusive voice of conscience in the community, it is no longer the exclusive instrument of charity or aid.

At least in the community where I live, all sorts of groups and organizations are into charity. Banks, schools, and professional baseball teams hold canned food drives for local food banks. All manner of organizations plan fund-raising runs, walks, and rides; and many of these take place on Sunday morning, which may represent some sort of vestige of the civic faith era: "Sunday morning is for good works." But this is not without a certain awkwardness and irony. I serve a downtown church, and one of the challenges we have these days is that there are so many fund-raising walks and runs scheduled to go through downtown streets on Sunday mornings that our church has to make special arrangements with the police so that people can get to the church!

My point is not that the church should cease to be an instrument of aid to the least fortunate. It is that the church has no lock — no monopoly — on this role today. People have discovered that they don't need the church to do such work. Indeed, those for whom worship is a priority may find themselves in the strange position of saying no to the AIDS, Breast Cancer, or March-of-Dimes walkathons, to charitable good works, because their Sunday mornings are committed to worship!

There are other problems with the church as the primary source or conduit of aid to the less fortunate. In much the same way that the church as the conscience of the community tends to moralize the faith, the church as conduit of assistance tends to distort the relationship between givers and receivers. Church people become the givers; the receivers are the other. *We* will help *them*. But the gospel does not provide such comfortable categories or safety. The gospel tends to tell us that we are they: we are all in need of grace; we all need forgiveness and mercy.

Another less than salutary effect of the church as source of assistance to the less fortunate has been to emphasize charity at the expense of justice. Food baskets every Christmas and Thanksgiving are a great gesture — just the thing for the church to do. But picketing local farmers and agribusiness concerns on behalf of a living wage for migrant workers is the church messing in politics! Sure, give a handout to homeless, mentally ill persons, but don't raise my taxes to provide mental health care that means people don't have to live on the streets!

Center of Community and Family Life

A third role of the church in the civic faith era was to be a center for community and family life. Here the community gathered for celebrations, rites of passage, and remembrances. In some way the church was often part of the great national holidays and festivals — Mother's Day, Memorial Day, the Fourth of July, Thanksgiving. And the church was the place where people went as a family: the church nurtured marriage and the family. "The family that prays together stays together!" Never mind that Jesus pretty much repudiated this thought when he told his mother and brothers, "Whoever does the will of God is my mother and my brother," and "I have come to set father against son, mother-in-law against daughter-in-law." In the civic faith era, a job of the church was to be a supportive place for families, for parents and their children, and to be the center of community life.

The reality of a postmodern, post-Christendom world is that it is multicentered. There is no one center of the community, at least not in many communities in North America today. There are many centers, and most people's lives are lived amid multiple loyalties. The school is one center, but the medical establishments are another; the library may be a kind of center, but so are the malls and other shopping areas. And there are multiple religious and cultural centers. For one sub-community, the mosque or synagogue is the religious center, while for others it is the cathedral, the neighborhood church, the home church, or the bookstore.

In the same way that there is no one normative center of the community, there is less sense today of a normative family configuration or that the church can limit itself to being a center for family life. And a closer reading of Scripture attunes the church to the way in which "family" can become a form of idolatry. Within a one-mile radius of the church I serve, forty-two percent of all residents are single adults. Thus the church that bills itself as "a family church or center" is sending a message that welcomes some but excludes others. This is not to say that the church will not be concerned to support parents, to form children in the faith, or to transmit the faith from generation to generation. That emphasis remains important; in fact, it has become a much greater challenge in a society where the generations tend to be defined over against one another. Nevertheless, the church as center of community and family life, as it was in the civic-faith era, is no longer an adequate model of the church's purpose.

In many ways the civic-faith-era church that did these things well — being the conscience of the community, providing aid and care to the least fortunate, and being a center of community and family life — had a strong and fitting ministry. But it was also a ministry that was so well adapted to the culture of North America, and specifically to small-town North America, that any sense of tension between gospel and culture was diminished or lost. It was difficult to tell any difference between a Christian way of life and the American and middle-class way of life. Being a Christian meant being a good American, a decent parent, a responsible citizen. That worked pretty well until people began to say to themselves, "If that's all it means, why do I need the church? Why go there?" Such questions, along with factors traced in chapter one, resulted in the exodus from the church of large numbers of my generation (the so-called "Boomers") who had been raised in the mainline Protestant churches. They did not leave for more conservative churches but to meld into secular culture.

Meanwhile, those who stayed often kept on with civic faith. But as society changed and become more secular, pluralistic, and postmodern, the church that clung to civic faith tended to look more and more like a kind of aging and antiquarian club. The old rhetoric of civic faith marched on, oblivious to changed realities. Amid this disjunction, the real purpose of such churches began to make them look like alumni groups or clubs. Indeed, as the civic-faith era has waned and the Protestant mainline has suffered precipitous and steady decline, one of the shapes the church has too often assumed has been that of a club or clan: while the rhetoric of civic faith remained the primary focus of the church, the purpose of the club became the care and satisfaction of its own members.

Kirk Hadaway has described this phenomenon well as a form of "goal displacement." The church, once founded and established to make a difference in the lives of others and in society, has in a time of change and confusion tended to adopt a diminished purpose and vision. Seeing or sensing that earlier roles and purposes — conscience of the community, instrument of aid, and center of the community — no longer quite worked, and yet unsure of other directions, too many churches have adopted as their implicit purpose the maintenance of a congenial community for their members. And the measure of a minister and church has become how well they keep the membership satisfied. As Hadaway points out, the experience of communion with God and service to others becomes secondary, if not lost altogether, as churches replace such purposes with those of being good social clubs — with a religious overtone — for their members. Too often this is what the congregations have become in the wake of the civic-faith era. No longer sure of their role or purpose, buffeted by social change, they have circled the wagons and gathered to meet their own needs for company and reassurance in the face of change and challenge.

If it is true that the church is no longer *the* conscience of the community, *the* instrument of aid to the least fortunate, or *the* center of community and family life, and if we recognize that faithfulness requires more of us than being a good social club for our members, what is the church's business today? Again, it is a time of wonderful opportunity for the church. The post-Christendom, postmodern era has given the church the opportunity to discover, or rediscover, a purpose more in keeping with its Scriptures and its own origins and formative years.

What is the church's purpose? I agree with those who argue that purpose is more important than vision. Often when things are going badly the church looks for a "visionary leader," someone who will come in and say, "There's the goal, the vision, the promised land. We need to head there." This tends to distort the role of the leader, or of leadership, turning it once again into an answer-providing agency and relieving the followers of responsibility. Moreover, it creates a kind catch-up mentality. We are always trying to become something other than what we are, to get somewhere we are not. In the short term it may be exciting; in the long term it tends to be tiring and discouraging. Vision has a place, but purpose is the more important question. What is the purpose of the church? I would argue that the shift that needs to be made is from civic faith (or its gone-to-seed expressions of church as club) to the "business" of human transformation. The purpose of the church is to bring about change in people's lives. Of course, to say that the purpose of the church is to bring about change in people's lives is inadequate on two counts; first, it does not spell out what kind of change; second, it makes too much of a claim for the church.

On the first count, the kind of change the church seeks to bring about can be further described in several phrases. We seek to "make disciples of Jesus." We are in the business of "Christian formation." We want to change people in such a way that the Christian story of grace and response becomes the lens, the perspective, through which they can see and understand all of life. And although mainline Protestant churches may be reluctant to use the word, what I am talking about is "conversion": turning around, being born anew, changed, made new, given a new heart and a new mind as we become followers of the One who makes all things new.

But while changing and transforming people in the light of God's story of grace may be the purpose of the church, this is ultimately God's work, not something the church does alone nor does by employing a four-, five-, or ten-step manual for success. Faith remains a gift, a gift of God. While the church may work at this change and contribute to it, and can provide an environment for it, neither the church nor its ministers make it happen. Only God — and God's grace — makes it happen, and often in ways that surprise and astonish the church and its ordained leaders.

Human Transformation

The purpose of the church today, a purpose much more in keeping with the purpose of the church in its earliest, pre-Christendom era, is that of human transformation. Our purpose is to change lives. As a pastor I find that one of the reasons that this is such a good time to be the church and to be a minister is that many people — and many of those who seek a church today — are seeking change in their lives. Gone is the era when people come to the church as a way of being part of the community or being good citizens. Where I live (Seattle and the Northwest) one is more likely to be, in some real sense, opting out of the majority community and prevailing expressions of citizenship by coming to church. According to current estimates, somewhere between 10 and 15 percent of people in Seattle attend a service of worship (any service of worship) in a given week. It is simply no longer the normal or expected thing to do.

I find that those who come to church today are often stimulated to do so by a crisis in their lives. That crisis may be the more ordinary and socially acceptable crisis of having children. But in Seattle having children is fast becoming a minority experience itself: the city is now second only to San Francisco among American cities in having the smallest percentage of its population under the age of eighteen. And while having children is an experience of blessing, it also has a way of rearranging people's lives and priorities — perhaps now more than ever. A new generation signals to parents that they are mortal, and the responsibility of being parents tends to make people reach for a larger story and set of meanings.

But often the crisis that brings people to church is something darker and more difficult: the suicide of a brother, the loss of a job, a divorce, depression, or a problem of substance abuse in one's own life or that of a family member. In the face of such crises, people experience vulnerability and disillusionment. They question the ways they have put life together up to that point. One way or another, many of those who seek the church today know that life is not working, that there is some brokenness or need in their lives and in our culture. In other words, people increasingly come to the church looking for change, for transformation, for healing, for a life that is deeper and more adventuresome than what they have found in the culture, where a kind of nihilism is covered over but not cured by affluence.

Increasingly today, I find that the leading-edge question that brings people to church is: "How can I have a spiritual life?" or "How can I get God in my life?" or "How can I be different?" These are not the questions of the civic-faith era. And to the extent that the church is primarily oriented to civic faith or has become a club, it will fail to address these kinds of questions. Too often the civic-faith church has met these questions with a committee assignment or a board position or with tepid "fellowship" that can be found as readily — perhaps better — elsewhere. Today more people are asking the kinds of questions and expressing the kinds of longings for which the church ought to be prepared to respond. The longings for depth, for meaning, for worship and spiritual practices that put a person in touch with the sacred, and for forms of engagement with others that are real and honest. To be sure, not all seekers want to pay the price that is required. There are those who want short-term highs, quick fixes, and whose patience for the long-term work of formation will quickly wear thin. Still, they are asking for what the church, at its most basic and essential, is about: communion with a higher power, with God, a spiritual life, a change, and healing. (In using the term "healing," I am not speaking primarily of the curing of mental or emotional illness, but of healing as a relationship with God, with self, and with others in a community of meaning and purpose.)

While affirming that God is the primary actor, the author of change and the transformation of people into disciples of Christ and citizens of God's realm and kingdom, how does the church go about accomplishing this purpose, and working in partnership with God and the Holy

Spirit? In subsequent chapters I will explore in greater detail what I think of as crucial forms of ministry for the church that is in the business of change and renewal. Here I wish to explore and affirm two further convictions that are crucial if we believe the church's business is to change people.

Do We Need Changing? Do We Need to Be Saved?

One of those convictions is that we do need change, or to put it in the language of faith and of the church, we do "need to be saved." Many today have grown up with different assumptions and convictions. Some have been taught to believe "I'm okay, you're okay": we don't need change, saving, or God. Many have been taught and led to believe that their highest duty and purpose in life is to be themselves and to be true to themselves. Clearly, there is some truth in self-awareness and the maxim "to thine own self be true." We do need integrity. But the contention that what we most need is to discover and be our true selves deserves closer examination.

In recent years, my wife and I have attended two college orientations, both at colleges that were historically church related but are now secular. Somewhere in the course of both orientations we heard college officials and faculty say something to this effect: "We are here, students, to teach you to think for yourselves, not to accept ideas just because someone says that you should. You have to make your own choices, determine your own values." I couldn't help thinking, So what else is new? These kids got that message with their mother's milk. It's the message of the whole culture: "It's up to you. There's nothing you can count on, nothing you can trust, rely on, turn to, or are accountable before — except yourself." We are here to teach method — critical thought — but not substance, not a body of thought, not a set of convictions or a way of life.

To put it another way, there is a doctrine of human nature at work here. It is the doctrine of the autonomous individual who depends on nothing but his or her inner resources. Philosophically, it is the bequest of Descartes, Rousseau, and Kant. Descartes taught us "I think, therefore I am." Rousseau promoted the idea that the individual was complete, competent, and good by nature; that precious self is corrupted by civilization and socialization and must be shielded from social pressures in order to flourish according to its own inner lights. To this Kant contributed the idea of moral autonomy and the conviction that morality is knowable by reason alone, independent of revelation.

The result is a doctrine of human nature that says that we are autonomous good selves who then become corrupted by family, socialization, and civilization. In many respects, this doctrine of human nature — with its autonomous individual — is at the root of profound personal and social problems. It encourages self-deception rather than honesty. It does not recognize the need for socialization, much less formation. It locates reality deep within, and it bends everything to one criterion: "Does this work for me?" But this is, from a Christian point of view, to take ourselves altogether too seriously, and not to take God nearly seriously enough.

The Christian faith operates from a quite different set of convictions about human nature. We are not autonomous individuals; we belong to God and are dependent on God. There is an Other, a power and reality beyond us, upon whom we may rely, in whom we can trust, and to whom we are accountable. Moreover, the gap between the goodness of God and troubledness of the world means that the self needs to be formed and reformed in order to flourish. Where modern culture has taught that it is enough to follow our own lights, Christianity has claimed that we are in need of formation and reformation of the self in order to conquer our *selves* and oppose those aspects of culture that deform us. This formative and re-formative work, this saving work, is God's work in Jesus Christ. We are not good by nature and corrupted by society, as modernity has maintained. We are flawed from the start and in need of formation and re-formation.

This can be put in another, perhaps more positive, way. The path of healing and transformation is the path of surrender. Freedom is found by letting go. This is, of course, a paradox — a gospel paradox. A culture that places such great emphasis on the individual will teaches us that freedom and peace come as we gain increasingly greater measures of power and control and are "in charge" of our lives. The gospel teaches that peace and true freedom — life — come by surrendering our selves, by seeing our illusions of control and autonomy for what they are, and by giving ourselves to God's love and purpose for our lives.

Many of those who stagger into a church today, reeling from one crisis or another, have discovered that they are not in control, and they have begun to sense the inadequacy of contemporary and prevalent understandings of the human being. They have begun to discover in their own lives that we humans are sinful creatures, capable of enormous self-deception. We need change, transformation, healing, saving. It is not saving that is solely or primarily for life hereafter, as fundamentalists would have it. But in contrast to many mainline and liberal church people, who assume that we are basically good and therefore need no change, we do need saving — a saving grace that may make us flourish in this life and in life beyond death.

Changed and Changing

As the church shifts from civic faith to human transformation, a second point needs to be made. The church is not the fellowship of those who have been fully and completely changed or saved and who require nothing more. In other words, the church is not the saved who are then to save others. The church is a fellowship, a gathering of those who are in the *process* of being changed, of those who are being saved and made new, and who invite others to join them in this adventure and in this life.

Put another way, the conversion we are about is like what Luther said about baptism: it is a once-in-a-lifetime experience that takes our entire lives to complete. Conversion may be crystallized in one of several key moments in a person's life, but it is also simultaneously a continual experience. We may "get it," but we don't "have it." Faith is a gift that requires continual care and renewal; it is not a possession we have in a fixed or permanent state. The implication of this is crucial for the life of a congregation. A congregation that is engaged in the work of human transformation does not hold a possession that it imparts to others. It participates in the ongoing work of God and invites others to share in it. It invites people to participate in a healing conversation, in the unfolding work of God for change and renewal of personal lives and of all creation.

What is the purpose of the church? Civic faith as the purpose of the church was right for a particular time; it was not wrong or bad. Civic faith becomes wrong insofar as it does not fit or engage a new time with different challenges. Today, in a new time, the purpose of the church and its ministries is more adequately described as transforming people in the light of God's grace — revealed in the Exodus, the Incarnation, and the Resurrection.

CHAPTER FOUR

From Assuming the Goods to Delivering the Goods

PART ONE: WORSHIP

Assuming the Goods in the Christendom Era

In the era of civic faith, when the mainline Protestant churches were the religious establishment of North American culture, we tended to assume that everyone was more or less Christian. Of course, we understood that there were Jews, but even they were related — sort of honorary Christians. The question in that era was not, as it is today, "Which faith, if any, are you?" but rather, "What kind of Christian are you — Protestant or Catholic?" If Protestant, what denomination — Methodist, Episcopal, Baptist, Presbyterian, etc.? While there was certainly regional and local variation in this perception, and certain churches and denominations protested such an understanding, there was a way during this period of American Christendom in which almost everyone, by virtue of being an American, was assumed to be a sort of Christian. By growing up in the culture you imbided the Christian faith — or so we thought!

A corollary of this perception of everyone being some sort of Christian was that everyone, therefore, had the basics. Everyone knew the Bible stories; everyone had some of the Christian hymns and songs; everyone understood the role of religious, i.e., Christian people, in founding America; and everyone knew the basics of Christian beliefs. All of this added up to churches tending to assume the goods, that is, to assume that people were, by virtue of being born and raised in North America, Christians, and that likewise people had and understood the basics of Christian faith and identity. You didn't have to do baptismal training; you seldom did adult baptisms. It would be curious to speak of "conversion": after all, how could you convert to what you already were — by birth and upbringing? Not only did Americans not require conversion, they did not need training in order to be Christians. When a new person shows up at church? Sign her up, and put her on a committee! She'll be fine!

In such a context, being a Christian tended to take on the lowest-common-denominator meaning of being a decent person and a good citizen. But as ours became an increasingly secular and religiously pluralistic society, many began to suspect, quite rightly, that one could be a decent person and a good citizen without being a Christian. If that's all it means to be a sort-of Christian, one certainly doesn't need the church for that, many concluded. In fact, the church, with its family-like squabbles and endless meetings, might increase the difficulty of being a decent person.

As I began my ministry in the late 1970s, I began to notice how shaky and inadequate these assumptions were. Not only did they define "Christian" in a way that was almost completely devoid of theological or biblical content, but they assumed that people who came to the church had certain basics, when in fact they often had nothing of the kind. They brought to the church a host of assumptions from secular culture and did not always take kindly to having these questioned or challenged. For example, worship, it was imagined, was primarily about getting some good advice, a few pointers, for making one's life better or easier, for improving one's family life or marriage, or rallying people to take the correct side on the issues or causes of the day. Don't bother me with theology! Don't confuse me with those weird parables! Don't tell me that Jesus was nonviolent! Sometime during those years, more promisingly, people for whom such a nominal and superficial religion had worn thin were beginning to come to church. As the years of my ministry have accumulated, I have noted that we can no longer assume the goods, and in many ways this is a wonderful development. Today those who come to church, especially in a place like the Pacific Northwest, often have had no religious or church background whatsoever. They come without the preconceptions or the nominal Christian faith of the Christendom era. Moreover, those I see coming to church today, seeking faith, are often prompted to do so by a crisis in their lives. Thus they come with questions, hungers, longings. Life as they have known it is not working. Something is wrong.

Delivering the Goods

In such a new and radically changed situation we can no longer assume the goods. The church must deliver the goods. I use the expression "deliver the goods" advisedly. In a real sense, only God can deliver the goods. Nevertheless, the church that plunks people on a committee, assumes that they have the basics, and serves up a bland and moralistic version of the Christian faith will probably not be addressing the deepest longings and questions that spur people to seek a church and faith in the postmodern era. "Delivering the goods" means that the church will pay particular attention to a few vital things. Among these are worship, the church's teaching ministry, and relationships with others that deepen faith. Together these three — worship, teaching, and community — are at the heart of Christian formation — of how Christ is formed in us, and how the church "makes disciples."

In the earlier time, the Christendom era, it would have come as news to many, even a shock, if the church had said, "You need formation" or "You need to be formed." "Aren't I already okay, as I am? Aren't I already sort of Christian?" No, answers the church today, you cannot be a Christian without formation, that is, without learning or training. The whole church is the formative agency, and its particular and crucial instruments of formation are worship, teaching, and Christian community.

In the balance of this chapter I will focus on the church's worship as the first and essential part of "delivering the goods." What's at stake for the church in worship? How can congregations strengthen their worship so that it does help to form and sustain people as Christian? What is the relationship of worship to a way of life and to Christian practices? In the next chapter I will continue with the theme of "delivering the goods" but will shift our attention to the teaching ministry of the church. Christian education, as it was focused primarily on children and youth and did so from a particular set of assumptions, was characteristic of the American Christendom era. Today we need to reclaim the language and understanding of Christian formation, and with it a new and reconceived teaching ministry for and by the whole church.

Worship as Encountering God

In the civic-faith church, worship was often a time to be reminded of our responsibilities as right-thinking people and good citizens. In other words, it was heavy on "shoulds." When it came to God, worship in the civic-faith era often tended to be less an experience *of* God than a reflection *about* God. To deliver the goods will mean, among other things, that worship is not first of all about what we should do but about what God has done and is doing. Nor will worship be "about God" in the sense that it is a kind of theology discussion group with options to consider. No, worship will invite people into an experience of the sacred, an encounter with God, one that is somehow life-changing.

There is an old, perhaps apocryphal, story about two signs that appeared one day on the sweeping green of the Boston Common. One said, "This way to lectures about God"; the second said, "This way to God." In the civic-faith era — and still in many mainline churches — the crowd (such as it is) is likely to follow the first sign. In the post-Christendom, postmodern era, people are increasingly inclined toward the direction of the second sign. They seek God, and they seek access to the sacred. In some ways this story might be taken as a kind of midrash on an encounter that occurs early in the third chapter of the Gospel of John. Under cover of darkness, a religious leader, Nicodemus, seeks out Jesus, evidently believing that he has followed the sign to "lectures about God." He attempts to engage Jesus in a discussion of how he was able to do what he was doing. But Nicodemus must have become confused and misread the sign: unwittingly he has followed the sign saying, "This way to God."

Jesus shows no interest in Nicodemus's attempt to pull back the curtain, nor in his appeal for an explanation, nor in a discussion of who he is and how he does the things he does. Jesus has something else in mind.

"You must be born anew from above," he tells Nicodemus. "You must be born again."

"What are you talking about?" stammers Nicodemus. "What can you possibly mean? Really, Jesus, I find all of this God stuff very fascinating, but I'm not up for a personal overhaul, or any kind of new birth — whatever that might mean!"

To be in the presence of God is to be in a zone of risk, of change, of reorientation, of new birth. This is what is centrally at stake in the worship of the church today. Will our worship be a lecture *about* God? Or will worship help us enter into that risky and life-giving dimension of God's presence where anything can happen, where we are not in control? Annie Dillard has it right when she says that the ushers at a worship service ought to be handing out hard hats and life jackets, not worship bulletins and smiles. To worship the God of Abraham and Sarah, Jacob and Rachel, Moses, Miriam, Mary, and Jesus is to risk change, new birth, and new life.

I identify with Nicodemus — especially as a preacher. In my first ventures in the pulpit, I imagined my task to be something like that of an Op-Ed columnist. I was to comment on issues of the day, throw in a little Scripture, and scatter some pearls of wisdom in the direction of the waiting congregation. I might have gotten away with this but for two things: my own inchoate longing for something more and deeper, and a remarkable teacher who asked insistently, "Are you listening to the text?" Under the tutelage of that teacher and other mentors, I began to catch the whiff of an altogether different kind of preaching — preaching that was less predictable, riskier, and much more exciting. This kind of preaching begins with the biblical text and with listening. Exegetical study, pastoral work, and my own life all became ways of listening for God through the lens of a particular text. It was risky if for no other reason than that I would not know what I was going to say before I preached. I had to wait — to listen for a word. Sometimes it came, clear and clean, like the sun on a bright winter day; but other times it was wrapped in mist and cloud, nearly obscure. But listening for God's word was different for me and for the congregation. It was alive. It was born of the encounter with God. Often I couldn't wait to share what I had heard.

But with time I found that my task as a preacher was not simply to share what I had seen or heard in my encounter with God's story. It was to help people hear, see, discover, and be discovered for themselves. Sometimes preaching is "Thus saith the Lord!" But more often it is helping people do their own listening for God. Instead of showing the slides, as it were, of my recent trip, it is acting as a guide for a river run of their own. When this kind of preaching happens, almost everyone gets wet. When the service is over, people are not nearly as likely to ask, "What was the sermon about?" or "What did the preacher say?" as they are to ask "What happened?" "What happened in there today?" When the service ends at quarter past twelve, they do not walk out the door to go home for lunch and watch a football game. They walk out into a new world, a world where Jesus Christ is Lord.

By beginning with this discussion of preaching, I do not mean to imply that worship is only or even primarily preaching. While I believe that preaching is critical and essential, it is but one element of worship. My point here is different: it is to say that worship is being in the presence of God, which, as Fred Craddock remarks somewhere, is a bit frightening. To be in the presence of God is what everyone wants, and it is also what everyone doesn't want.

My hunch is that unless the preacher is willing to enter that zone of risk and new life, the congregation is unlikely to go there either. In worship we have to do with an Other, who may kill us in order that we may truly live. We risk this in worship so that, over time, we may come to see and know that in all of life we have to do with this Other, this holy, mysterious, merciful, and surprising God, who regularly eludes our control and whose ways are not our ways. Whether or not our worship calls and invites us into God's transforming presence is the crucial question facing the once mainline churches. There is no one way that this happens, nor is there any one style of worship or method that will guarantee that it will. There is no form of worship, no order of service, no liturgical pattern or practice that ensures the Holy Spirit will show up. There are, however, angles of approach, starting places, and foundational convictions that make worship — as the act of being in the presence of God who brings the dead to life — more or less likely.

Of the four congregations that I have served, two have had some version of the worship pattern and the split that has become common in many congregations. There was a "traditional" service and a "contemporary" one. Of the two congregations with this worship pattern, one had taken the thing to its logical extreme. That church offered five worship services, or "experiences," but not because the sanctuary of the church was overflowing. Far from it: it was less than half full. But each service appealed to a different taste. Two of the five featured a sermon, while two others featured congregational discussions, and one a children's story. For two the music was strictly classical and led by an organ; for two it was folk and contemporary, led by a guitar; for the fifth, there was no music at all.

There is nothing intrinsically wrong with this plurality of services or worship formats. There is nothing to say that each cannot call and invite people into the presence of God, nothing except the assumption that so frequently underlies such a pattern, that underlies a great deal of worship in the mainline Protestant church today: that the worshiper is a customer, a client, and that good worship meets the needs of the customer. Therefore, if your religious taste runs to Bach chorales and a twenty-minute sermon, this one's for you. If, however, guitar strumming and an open mike are more to your liking, try this one. And so on.

There is, of course, as in all heresies, a grain of truth in this approach. People do have different backgrounds, preferences, and tastes. Cultures vary. Communication of any form, including communication of the gospel, requires respect for the background and sensitivity of the hearers. Yet when the main question asked of worship becomes, "Did it meet my needs?" or "Was I comfortable?" we may be on shaky ground. What we are doing begins to look less like church, which is called into existence and sustained by a Word not our own, and more like a religious club. Worship leaders and planners begin to ask, "What will work?" meaning "What will people like?" No worship leader or planner can be oblivious to such questions. Neither, however, can those be the guiding questions. Such questions almost inevitably result in our making ourselves the focus and object of worship. Rather than asking, "Was God glorified and truly and rightly praised?" or "Was the church reminded of its source and identity and destiny?" or "Did we encounter God?" the questions become, "Was I pleased? Edified? Entertained? Were my needs met?" At some level, however, the gospel does not wish to meet our needs so much as to redefine them. The gospel does not intend to "connect" to our world, but to change our world.

The misdirected assumptions and questions that I have described may be most clearly evident in those churches with varied worship "options" and "experiences," but they surely can be equally pervasive where there is no plurality of services or styles. When pastors take their task to be one of pleasing the congregation, they are on thin ice: worship is wrong in its inception, flawed from the beginning. Often the result is worship that is simply trivial — an activity without the height, breadth, or depth of the gospel.

To help people grasp the difference in approach and basic convictions, I have often turned to Kierkegaard's description of worship as theater. In one way of looking at worship, the actors are the preacher, the choir, the liturgists, and musicians. The audience is then the congregation, which settles into its place to be touched, badgered, inspired, or entertained by the actors on stage. But to view worship in this way, Kierkegaard points out, is to misconceive worship. Its flaw is betrayed by the question, "Where is God?" Nowhere to be found! Which is precisely what is wrong all too often in the church's worship. But reframe the theater of worship in the following way: the actors in the worship drama are the members of the congregation. Worship leaders are just that — leaders and prompters of the congregation's worship of God. The choir does not perform; it leads the people's singing of praise to God. The preacher does not dazzle the congregation with her wisdom; she leads the congregation into God's presence. Where is God in Kierkegaard's reconceived theater of worship? God is the audience for the church's worship. God has become the object and the focus of our worship, not ourselves.

The questions we ask, now, as we leave the theater of worship are different. They are not first of all, "Was I pleased?" "Was I comfortable?" "Were my needs met?" Rather, we ask, "Did I worship — did we worship — God?" "Was God present?" "Was the Holy Spirit at work?" "Was God rightly praised?" "Has faithfulness been encouraged by our worship, and do we see it demonstrated in the lives of this people?"

Kierkegaard's revised theater of worship makes it clear that worship is less a noun than a verb. It is not something we go to and watch or that happens at a particular hour each week. It is something we do, an event in which we take part. This is the meaning of the Greek word *leitourgia,* or liturgy: "the work of the people of God." It does not mean, as it so often seemed to be interpreted in the liturgical innovations of the 1960s and 70s, that the ordained simply step aside and turn the planning and leadership of worship over to the laity. Nor does it mean that no worship service can be valid without a sprinkling of laypeople involved in tasks such as reading Scripture or praying. It means that worship is something in which we, the church, actively participate, whether we are in the chancel or the nave, and God is the object and the focus of our worship.

Kierkegaard's theater of worship gets God back in the picture. Our prayer and our singing are speaking to and of our God. Our preaching leads us into a risky encounter with a God, whose ways are not our ways and whose thoughts are not our thoughts. Our sacraments are God at work in our midst to name, claim, nurture, wash, and feed us. And our worship is the church's dangerous attempt to let God be God.

Worship as Congregational Formation

If Kierkegaard's analogy of worship to theater is helpful and instructive, it may also be misleading. God as the audience for our worship may suggest a certain divine passivity: a watchful but distant and unengaged God. Yet we discover in worship that even as we focus our worship on God and lose ourselves in God's love and praise, and as we give ourselves to God in offering and sacrament, something also happens to us and for us. Even as we are busy praising God, God is busy healing, touching, renewing, shaking, and redeeming us. Perhaps it is something like athletes, musicians, or teachers giving themselves wholly to their sport, music, or teaching. Or like children who are lost in play: even as they give, they do receive. As they lose themselves in the game, the song, or the subject, they are found.

There are two particular and crucial ways that we find ourselves anew and receive in worship, even as we give ourselves to it. A congregation, which may be a close and caring group where everyone knows everyone else, or may be a collection of strangers or simply a crowd, gains a new identity in worship. They become a people, the people of God. They become church. Worship is primarily about God and being in the presence of God. But it is not only that; it is also about congregational formation. And it is about identity: in worship we are hard at work forming a people. We are constantly reminding ourselves and being reminded of the meaning of our baptism, of our peculiar identity and vocation as church.

For many years the church, the mainline Protestant churches especially, did not think that we had to work very hard at this. We did not imagine that we needed to be concerned about this because we could rely on the culture to do our work for us. The necessary tension between church and culture had been relaxed — had gone limp. We did not worry much about how a new generation got the stories, the songs, the sacraments, or the particular perspective on life they conveyed because we believed that being an American and being a Christian were pretty much the same thing. Alan Ehrenhalt's book *The Lost City*, subtitled "The Forgotten Virtues of Community," is a study of three Chicago-area communities in the 1950s. In the section on Elmhurst, a Chicago suburb, Ehrenhalt describes a fairly typical aspect of life in America two generations ago. The Jaycees (Junior Chamber of Commerce) were "the nerve center of the new suburban generation." "In December the Jaycees launched a 'Put Christ Back in Christmas' campaign, crusading against the 'Xmas' vulgarization and the creeping secularism it represented. In the winter of 1953, there were 'Put Christ Back in Christmas' stickers and signs all over Elmhurst — on postal machines, on bushes, on every tree sold for the holidays anywhere in town. Residents were urged to send cards that had only a religious theme, and merchants were pressured to place biblical scenes in their store window. The Boy Scouts were enlisted to distribute 8,000 pamphlets door-to-door, explaining the significance of the crusade."

That was the world of my childhood. The church, especially the mainline Protestant church, was the established religion of American culture. For better or worse — and I believe it is for the better — we no longer live in that world. The church is no longer supported or sanctioned by the culture. Community campaigns, Boy Scouts, and public school programs no longer transmit the Christian faith. There is a greater tension between Christ and culture than we had once imagined.

If the primary issue at stake for worship today is the presence of God, the second issue at stake is the formation of congregational identity, the formation of the church. And neither will this be done for us by the culture at large any longer. In the New Testament we find the apostle Paul, founder and nurturer of congregations, especially focused on this task. Paul was forever reminding the early Christian congregations of their baptism into Christ, of its significance, of their new identity, and that they were no longer the people they had once been. Only after his labored explanations about identity, about who we are, does Paul turn to ethics, to how we are to act.

In this ongoing work of remembering and becoming who we, by God's grace, are, we do strange things in worship — at least things the world counts as strange. We read from a book whose stories are two and three thousand years old. A person, a live human being, usually without the support of makeup, special lighting, visual props, or background music, stands up to interpret these stories and their meaning for the community today. Generally these preachers go on for longer than the "average human attention span" dictated by the television and video generation. Clearly, this is strange. Moreover, we do things like pour water over people, washing adults and children, and saying "Now, you belong to God."

Most Sundays I look out on a congregation that includes people from both the city's homeless shelters and its wealthy suburbs. I see traditional (so-called nuclear) families, and I see gay and lesbian couples — plus quite a few widows. I see people who are fantastically successful by the world's standards, and I see people who are struggling with mental illnesses. And I say, "We are all one in Christ Jesus." On the face of it, this is a rather odd, even incredible, statement. More improbably, we often seem to believe that it is true, that this is who we really are. On those Sundays when someone is baptized, when the congregation is invited to renew its baptismal vows, I say to successful attorneys, corporate executives, people who are poor or sick, children, and any others who present themselves: "You are a child of God, a disciple of Christ, and a member of the Church. Remember your baptism and be thankful." The world's distinctions are set aside, transcended, and people are renamed.

We gather around a table where all are fed and all have enough not that we may be told, "This is the way the world is supposed to be," but rather, "This is the way the world really is. Now, here, in this sacrament, you are seeing the truth, glimpsing reality. Our is-ness precedes our ought-ness. Mission begins here in worship with the naming of a new identity, the creation of a new people."

My friend Will Willimon tells the story of worshiping with a black congregation during the Civil Rights struggle. He and others like him, white students who had come from schools in the north, grew impatient with the services of worship that seemed to go on forever.

"Enough worship," they said. "Let's get out of here. Let's get on with it, with the real thing."

"Hold on just a minute," said their African-American hosts. "We have been at this longer than you have. When you go out there, and they let the dogs loose and open up the fire hoses, you'll need to know who you are and whose you are. You'll need to know that you are God's child, that you are walking with Jesus."

Thus worship, at least in part, is the constant reiteration of a new identity, a new vision. It is not leaving the "real world" for the unreality or escape of a stained-glass hour. It is entering the real world and seeing ourselves and others as we really are, as God sees us. We leave this act with new sight, new hearing, new hearts. We are newly prepared to engage the powers of this world. In order for worship to do this, it must be different from and more than the frequently "head-first" experience that it has become in many mainline Protestant congregations. Our historic respect for the mind and the intellect is a strength and a virtue. But like all virtues, when pushed too far or too single-mindedly, it becomes a vice. Worship becomes arid, abstract, and disembodied. For the Hebrews, the heart was the center of the human being. It represented not only the emotions but the whole person — intellect, emotions, will, and senses. If worship is to form people in a new identity and to form a new people, it will need to speak to the heart, to the whole person, and not only to the intellect.

Worship as Training in Spiritual Practices

If "delivering the goods" in worship is first about the presence of God, and second about formation and identity in the church, it is also about training people in the central practices that form and constitute a Christian way of life. Like much of life's important instruction, this training in spiritual practices through worship is indirect. In worship we do not, for the most part, say, "We will now learn how to pray." We simply pray. We listen as others pray. We sing, and perhaps we begin to notice that our hymns are sung prayers. Nor do we often say "We will now instruct you in offering." Rather they watch ten- and eleven-year-olds proudly carry forward the bread they have baked for Communion, laying it on the table before God and the congregation. We listen as another speaks of the meaning of their offering and how they think about money and its place in their lives. We bring our own gifts forward and lay them before God, learning to offer by offering.

Today there is a new interest in the practice of spirituality — spiritual disciplines such as contemplative prayer and fasting. People are going on spiritual retreats and seeking the counsel of spiritual directors. All of this is fine, but it may cause us to overlook the way in which worship is a focused experience of the central practices that characterize a Christian life. In this sense, worship is a kind of weekly dress rehearsal, a practice of the steps and moves and postures that are a part of the dance of being a person of faith in the world each day.

Often, for example, worship begins with some sort of praise. Whatever its form (organ voluntary, flower arrangement, dance, litany, hymn of adoration), praise tends to challenge our natural self-centeredness. It reminds us that truth and reality lie far beyond us, even as they are at work within us. The praise of God invites us to cease our frequent preoccupation with ourselves, to attend to something larger, and to the grace and generosity we ourselves have received. Over against the world where we become accustomed to taking life for granted, or occasionally begrudged, through the practice of praise we learn that life is an astonishing gift.

Likewise, confession of sin in worship is a practice that challenges our tendency toward self-justification and judgment of others. We are reminded as we engage in this practice that "all have sinned and fallen short of the glory of God." We hear that we are justified, not by our achievements, but by God's free grace. In the midst of a culture committed to self-esteem, we learn to think of ourselves in an odd way — as "sinners" who are forever making either too much or too little of ourselves. We learn, in our confession of sin, to tell the truth about ourselves, about our brokenness, and our need for grace. We learn that nothing can separate us from God, not our successes or our failures. It is a spiritual practice with implications for all of life and for living as a disciple of Christ.

One might, in fact, consider worship as a set of practices, as training to be Christian. In worship we learn the steps in the dance that constitute being Christian, and we rehearse them over and over, so that over time they may become second nature to us. These practices include keeping the Sabbath, forgiveness, hospitality, listening for God, prayer, offering, sacrament, and blessing. Each in its own way is a complex spiritual practice that is intended to form us as Christians. Each one makes a different claim. Every time, for instance, that we give money away as an offering to God, we say in effect that the way to overcome the insistent voices that chant "Never enough, never enough" is not to hoard but to give. By sharing, giving, offering, we learn that we have enough. It is, like so much of the Christian faith, a paradox. As a woman of my church said recently, "Stewardship is a violation of common sense."

If worship is, by and large, indirect instruction in the spiritual practices of a Christian life, there is also a time and place for more direct instruction. Much of the catechesis of the early church was training to participate in worship. Our catechesis, our teaching ministry today, might well reclaim this as one of its central tasks. Every year, one of the best-attended classes in my congregation is the one on "Worship and the Sacraments." We explore what is going on in worship: What are its origins? Where have the patterns of worship, or liturgy, come from? How are the various elements that make up a service related? I have found that people are eager for this kind of teaching, and they are pleased to discover that in worship we are being formed and instructed in the practices and perceptions at the heart of Christian life everywhere and always.

Strengthening Worship

"Okay," you may be thinking, "this has been helpful, but how are we to proceed? If worship at my church is to invite people into God's transforming presence, to form a new people, and to engage people in the spiritual practices that constitute a Christian life, how do we go about it? Where do we go from here?"

This cannot, of course, be reduced to a series of steps to implement or methods to follow — in part because there is significant variety in congregational settings and cultures. The general themes and orientation that I have suggested will take on flesh and blood in a variety of ways in different congregations. Nor can it be reduced to steps or methods precisely because God refuses to be programmed, and the Holy Spirit blows where it wills. Yet, though we cannot suggest a prescribed set of steps or a methodology, it is possible to suggest directions and possibilities for clergy and congregations who wish to strengthen worship. I have come up with the seven below.

Some years ago, while serving New York's Riverside Church, Ernie Campbell offered the suggestion that instead of trying to plan the extraordinary, we do well to "energize the ordinary." Sometimes worship renewal has meant more bells and whistles, balloons and banners. This betrays a lack of confidence in the ordinary to be the vessel of the extraordinary. It's better to take the ordinary elements of worship and vivify them, do them well, and trust them as instruments of God's grace and presence.

Something that helps congregations and clergy vivify and do the elements of worship well is *the study of worship.* Start with basic questions: What is worship? Why worship? What is the origin of our pattern and practices of worship? How do the different parts of a service form an integrated whole? What is the role of music in worship? What are the sacraments and why do we celebrate them? Where do the Scriptures that are read in worship come from? Who selects them, and on what basis? What is the purpose of the sermon? What helps us to prepare for worship? There are a host of helpful books and articles that can inform such study and exploration. In recent years many Protestant denominations have created new books of worship. Often their introductory sections are substantive and useful for congregational study. The important thing, in a process of renewal, is to revisit basic questions, assumptions, and information. In many once-mainline congregations, such questions and exploration may not have occurred in living memory.

Second, worship that would have God at its center will be *rooted in the Scriptures.* This does not mean that the preaching becomes labored exposition of texts or that all liturgical elements are drawn directly from Scripture. It does mean that the perceptions and perspectives of worship leaders and planners — as well as the congregation — are increasingly formed by the Scriptures and not by the personal preferences of the preacher or the civic calendar of Mother's Day, the Fourth of July, and Labor Day. This is critical because the Scriptures are consistent in directing us toward God. They are our best defense against worship that lacks God's presence. The Common Lectionary is a great help here, providing an ecumenically agreed-on pattern for the selection of Scripture for worship. But even then, the important thing is not "sticking to the Lectionary," but being formed in and by the theocentric nature of the Scriptures themselves.

The Common Lectionary is also helpful as worship leaders seek to plan services that resemble a well-coordinated meal rather than a smorgasbord of options. Use of a lectionary is one way to integrate sermon, music, sacraments, and prayers, and thus to provide a congregation in the midst of an often-fragmented world with worship that has a sense of wholeness and integrity. Too many services of worship seem to be some kind of smorgasbord. There may be a pattern, but it is often simply a linear rather than an organic pattern, in which elements are woven together in a complementary way. Many of the newer hymnals are helpful here by providing indexes to the Lectionary and to Scripture.

Third, while we desire an organic quality in worship — a sense of wholeness — this does not mean that there can be no *diversity* in a given service. In fact, drawing music from diverse genres is important today. Some variety in the ways the Word is proclaimed is appropriate, too, as is variation in the way the sacraments are celebrated. As an example of the latter, on certain Sundays in the congregation I serve, Communion is served in the customary style of the Reformed churches, that is, in the pews. This form emphasizes that God's grace seeks us even before we seek it. Other times, we celebrate Communion at tables, drawing on the Passover and Upper Room narratives. And still other Sundays, the congregation comes forward for Communion, a form that emphasizes the way in which the sacrament is a response to the proclamation of the good news. This is a mindful diversity, rooted in Scripture and theology.

Today we are often tempted to deal with the shifting of eras and paradigms by some appropriation of the "traditional" and "contemporary" dichotomy. A better direction is *diversity within services.* So, for example, one might begin the service with one of the great structural hymns of the English or German heritage, but then later in the service sing a folk or gospel hymn, and still later a more structural but contemporary hymn. Avoid the traditional/contemporary dichotomy because it tends to hallow our earthen vessels rather than God's transcendent power (II Corinthians 4).

A fourth strategy for strengthening worship is to connect the dots between *worship and ethics,* but to do so lightly. What are the implications of sharing the bread for our way of living in the world, or the implications of the offering for our use of money, or the implications of baptism for the kind of community we are to become? Ethics — how we are to live and behave — flows out of who we are, out of our identity, which is what worship is continually describing and redescribing: "You are the Body of Christ; therefore, be who you are." Today it is important to build the connection between worship and ethics at this basic level and to avoid, with some exceptions, direct ethical instruction or exhortation. Generally speaking, it seems important to help people find the path without telling them what to see as they walk it.

An important tool for finding the path is *the liturgical year.* It is, along with other tools we have mentioned, such as the lectionary, one tool for helping congregations deepen their faith and their distinctive identities as Christians. Every community orders time somehow, and we all live in a society that has its own way of ordering — and sometimes disordering — time. The seasons of the Christian year help to bring certain themes consistently and regularly to the fore at particular times of the years, while others recede. They provide a tool for persons and families who seek to connect their personal and home devotional life to the larger story. The seasons of the year keep before us the core story of the Christian faith. And the church year becomes a basis for introducing varied season-related elements in music, colors, and liturgy.

For congregations whose worship is sermon centered, a new emphasis on the *sacraments and rituals* of the church provides worship that is more holistic, that involves the body as well as the mind, and that is not just head first. My sense is that people long for the space that good ritual provides for their imaginations and emotions. Moreover, in a time of shifting cultures and paradigms, the experiences in worship that speak to our nonrational and unconscious being become more important instruments of worship, healing, and conversion. Many mainline churches have minimized the sacramental element, perhaps because they distrust matter and are more comfortable with ideas. But this has resulted in an imbalance of worship and faith.

Seventh, and finally, the *attitude and convictions of congregational leadership* are crucial. The ordained clergy must believe worship is central and that it matters if it is to become of central importance to a congregation and its members. A congregation's lay leaders must be encouraged to give time to understanding worship, to preparing for the parts they play in leadership (from ushering to greeting, from choral music to prayer). And a pastor's preaching, praying, and leading must flow from the conviction of the centrality of God's presence and of the power of the Holy Spirit to bring about renewal.

CHAPTER FIVE

Delivering the Goods

PART TWO: FROM CHRISTIAN EDUCATION
TO CHRISTIAN FORMATION

In the era of American Christendom, one seldom, if ever, heard the word "formation" or the phrase "Christian formation" in mainline Protestant churches. We spoke of "Christian education"; we had "education buildings" or wings; and people were employed as "Christian educators." And when we spoke of "Christian education," everyone knew that it meant a program focused on children and youth. The prevailing pattern in mainline and civic faith congregations has been that the teaching ministry, or Christian education, was primarily for children, while worship was for adults. This reflects the Christendom-era assumption that most people had the basics, or that they got them in Sunday school. Today, while the teaching ministry with children continues to be important, the church must focus with equal motivation and vigor on adults. Instead of 10-15 percent of a congregation's adults involved in some form of teaching ministry, the church today ought to expect a figure more in the neighborhood of 75-80 percent of adults involved in ongoing teaching and learning themselves. Moreover, the overall ministry of teaching needs to be seen as one part of the larger work of Christian formation.

The new use of the old word "formation" is a way of acknowledging that, in this new time, being and becoming Christian is more than an exercise in accumulating information. It is the shaping — the formation — of a particular kind of person. Christian formation includes what we have thought of as more formal teaching, or ordered learning; but it also includes a host of less formal or didactic formative experiences.

During the era of American Christendom, the Sunday school was the church's primary "educational strategy," according to C. Ellis Nelson. But he argues that today the congregation itself is the primary educational strategy, a community that is engaged in formation in every aspect of its life. This move, from Sunday school to congregation, reflects the shift from Christian education to Christian formation.

In reflecting on his own confirmation in the 1960s, Martin Copenhaver makes the following observations. "The model of Christian education that was reflected in my confirmation class experience assumed that we were already Christians, not by virtue of our baptisms, or even because we were nurtured in the church. Rather it was assumed that we were already Christians because, how could we not be? If you are growing up in what is presumed to be a Christian land, if the Christian faith seems to be in the very water you drink and in the air you breath, does the question even need to be asked?"

Christian education was for those who were already Christian, those who were Christian by virtue of growing up in North America. Formation recognizes that we are not Christian by virtue of growing up or simply living in this society. We need to be formed in the ways, values, stories, and perceptions of a different worldview. Copenhaver provides a further helpful summary of contrasts between education and formation, none of which, he emphasizes, ought to be pushed too far, but which help us to see the differences.

First, the purpose of Christian education is to inform; by contrast, the purpose of Christian formation — as the word itself implies — is to form, to shape, to mold.

Second, Christian education engages the intellect; by contrast, Christian formation engages the whole person.

Third, the goal of Christian education is understanding; by contrast, the goal of formation is faithfulness.

Fourth, Christian education can be pursued in settings dedicated to that purpose (such as classrooms); by contrast, Christian formation cannot take place in isolation. Indeed, Christian formation takes place in the complex and dynamic context of the entire life of the community of faith. To put it another way, Christian formation is the whole person molded in the context of the whole community. It is life lived in the round.

Fifth, Christian education can take place in fairly straightforward ways. We know a lot about how to dispense information. It follows predictable patterns. Progress can be measured. By contrast, how Christian formation takes place is harder to trace. Because formation depends heavily on the work of the Holy Spirit, it is not nearly as predictable. In most instances, we are reduced to saying something like this: Christian formation often seems to happen in this kind of setting, when these elements are present. That is, it is harder to trace fully how one is formed than it is to trace how one is educated.

Clearly, the ways and setting of Christian formation are many. It is in a real sense the work of the whole community of faith. In what follows, however, I will focus on five particular ways to be engaged in Christian formation and to deliver, rather than assume, the goods: (1) congregation as teacher; (2) ordered learning; (3) Christian formation of children; (4) ministries of service and witness; and (5) small groups.

Congregation as Teacher

In the era when church and culture formed a more or less seamless whole, we were less aware of the congregation as an alternative community and way of life. But today, the congregation does represent and embody, however imperfectly, an alternative perception and way of life. Thus, in a real sense, the church teaches in everything it is and does. For example, we teach about the place and significance of Scripture by how it is read in worship, by how it is treated in sermons, and by the place it holds in our daily lives. Is it primary or secondary, essential or incidental? Is it treated casually or as vital?

Or to draw on another example, the church teaches the practice of hospitality by how we welcome, or do not welcome, the stranger. Recently, our congregation was asked to welcome a convicted sex offender, now released from prison, to worship among us. This precipitated a particular challenge to our practice of hospitality, but also an occasion for discernment: how could we fulfill our obligation to be safe for children and other vulnerable persons among us, and yet welcome the sinner? Not only did the congregational discussion of these issues provide an occasion for considering our practice of hospitality and its scriptural and theological sources, but the process of discernment itself became an occasion in which the congregation taught its particular way of reaching a decision. Our resolution attempted to honor two scriptural convictions: protection of the vulnerable and welcoming of sinners.

The congregation teaches about matters large and small by the way it lives and practices its faith. Do we pay attention to issues of justice in our community, or do we ignore them? Do we pray for communities and people other than ourselves or not? How do we pray? Is all prayer led by ordained ministers, or can laypeople pray in a powerful way?

When, during the civic-faith era, the overlap between church and society was greater, it was less true that the church taught by all that it said and did. Today, when going to church represents, at least in my city, a departure from the norm, the church teaches in everything it does.

Ordered Learning

To begin with the more or less formal teaching ministry of the church, it has been my observation that, in the civic-faith churches, the kinds of classes that are offered for adults tend to be of the "side dish" variety. That is, the menu for adult education offerings is often filled with whatever is of current interest, whether a particular social issue is compelling that year or a new spiritual practice has caught people's fancy. Sometimes what the church has offered under the rubric of "adult education" has no theological or biblical content at all. It is something that could just as well have been offered at the community center down the street, or the senior club, or the local community college.

Today, as the church seeks to deliver the goods, we find that more and more people come to church looking for what the church might reasonably be expected to offer. Programs such as biblical study, courses in Christian theology, and opportunities to develop spiritual practices such as prayer, discernment, or exploring the implications of faith for being a parent. In this new situation, where there is a real hunger for what might be "faith development" or "spiritual growth," the church will do well not to offer side dishes but rather the main courses of Christian faith and practice. There are a number of ways to go about this. Indeed, the task of planning such a program of ordered learning may itself prove a powerful educational and formative experience for a congregation or a task force.

One option is to make Bible study central in the life of the church. There are several programs available for this, such as the Kerygma and Bethel courses. Alternately, the lectionary texts can be used for congregation-wide Bible study. This has the advantage of preparing people for worship and reinforcing the study experience in the worship experience. This format can be further built on if the congregation is using a lectionary-based curriculum in its teaching ministry with children and youth. For either of these options, the training and support of leaders will be a crucial component.

Another option for delivering the goods in this new time is to plan a core curriculum of Christian faith and practice. What are the things that we believe Christians ought to know? Our congregation has developed what we call "Wednesday Night Live": each Wednesday we offer one or more courses in each of four different tracks: Scripture, Theology, Spiritual Life and Practices, and Christian Ethics. The particular courses change, but the tracks continue to ensure coherence and balance. Some of the courses are foundational and are periodically repeated. Examples of foundational courses include, "Introduction to the Bible," "The Old Testament," "The New Testament," "Christianity 101," "Prayer for Beginners," "Christian Ethics," "My Faith and My Job." Other classes might be considered elective and are less likely to be repeated. In recent years these have included courses such as "The Book of Jeremiah," "Augustine's Confessions," "Faith and Parenting," and "Bioethics."

However a particular congregation puts its own "ordered learning" together, the point is that the "goods" can no longer be assumed, but must be taught and delivered. And the goal of such teaching and learning is not simply to share information. It is to be about the work of formation, of shaping and molding people in a particular worldview and way of life.

Christian Formation of Children

The pattern of an earlier era, as noted above, was education for children and worship for adults. Both children and adults need both — worship and teaching ministry. Or better, both require formation in which the church as a whole is at work, in manifold ways, relying on the Holy Spirit to form a people. This does, however, entail some shifts and new directions in the church's ministry with children. One is that children and youth need to participate fully in the central formative event of the church's life, its worship. For too many years, children were either not present at all in the church's worship or they were dismissed after a brief "appearance." Often that appearance was at a "children's sermon" or "children's moment." While some congregations and pastors have done this well, it has too often proved to be a manipulation of children for adult entertainment. Better than the children's sermon or singling children out in a kind of Art Linkletter redux is to include children in ways that introduce them to the church's worship and teaches them to participate in it. Children can participate as worshipers and as worship leaders in almost all aspects of the church's worship. Indeed, it may be less of a problem for children than for adults who have come to expect that worship is primarily an intellectual experience. The presence of children can help a congregation reclaim a more full-orbed worship, one that is worshiping God not only with the mind but with the heart, the body, and the senses as well.

Inclusion in worship is one crucial element in including children in the whole life of the Christian community. Another important tool is the use of mentors with young people, perhaps during Confirmation. The task of a mentor is to get to know that specific adolescent, to hear his or her hopes and questions, to share experience within the life of the church together, and to share something of his or her own faith with the young person — what has shaped it and how it is lived out. We have known for a long time that faith is formed in and by relationships. God, after all, did not send us in Jesus a program, but a person. A mentor relationship for teens builds on this insight at a crucial transitional moment in the life of the young person.

As the church seeks to do formative work with children and teens, another opportunity is offered by ministries of service. Recent work by the Minneapolis-based Search Institute have shown how crucial it is to the faith growth and formation of children and teenagers to participate alongside their parents and other adults in service and mission work. As part of our congregation's ministry of connecting people with opportunities to serve their neighbors in need and so practice discipleship, we identify particular opportunities that are appropriate for a family to do together. Some of these have included packing bags of food for the hungry, serving a meal at a shelter, or being pen pals with children at a church in another part of the world.

Ministries of Service and Witness

"I have concluded," writes Martin Copenhaver, "that we need to approach ministries of service as opportunities for Christian formation, without apology and with great expectation. Of course, we have always known that service in the name and Spirit of Christ has formative power. Many of us can point to times when we were given the opportunity to serve as perhaps the most formative experiences of all. But I think we have been largely apologetic about that, as if that formation were an unintended and extraneous by-product."

In his reflection on ministries of service and witness as powerful formative experiences, Copenhaver points to the way that people will often report, sheepishly, that they have actually received much more than they gave in the experience. And somehow that seems to be illegitimate. But perhaps a way to acknowledge that one of the reasons we engage in ministries of service, to encounter God and in the process be formed and refashioned, is to speak of such ministry as "the exchange of gifts."

Copenhaver goes on to tell the story of a recent experience in his own congregation in regard to a capital funds drive. Members of the congregation began to speak of the fund drive as "for ourselves," saying, "We need to do something for others." Such a dichotomy is frequent in the civic-faith congregation. "Some of us," writes Copenhaver, "began to learn about the tremendous need for small residences for adults with mental retardation. Such residences, when fully integrated into local communities, provide a much-needed alternative to the large, institutional residential programs.

"There was no such residence in our town, so we bought a property and, with a partner organization with experience in serving adults with MR, we opened a house. As we began to work with folks with MR in general, and the four residents who eventually moved into the house in particular, it became very clear that any distinctions between givers and receivers just didn't apply. We began to talk, quite straightforwardly, about the ways in which we all benefit from this ministry of service.

"We talked about the ways in which those of us who seem to prize competence and intellect above all, benefit greatly from relationships with those who manifest the kind of joy, love, and other gifts of the Spirit that are not dependent on competence or intellect. In short, we were beginning to recognize what our Scriptures have long taught us: God has blessed the poor, the sick, and the vulnerable, so we want and need to be near them. We have much to gain and to learn from being with those God holds especially dear. In short, in such interactions we encounter God. Which is another way of saying that it is a setting for the most profound kind of Christian formation."

Small Groups

One of the most powerful tools of formation, and one that has been re-discovered in a variety of settings, is the small group. From "twelve-step" programs to Weight Watchers to youth programs, small groups have emerged as one of the best tools of formation. In such groups, people seek to encourage and support the formation and transformation of other people. Groups are generally made up of those engaged in the same work of change; some are just beginning, while others may be further along the path. But they all are clear that change and transformation — formation of new lives and behaviors — is what they are about. All are clear, moreover, that the responsibility for this work is in the person himself or herself — and "a higher power." The group provides models, support, accountability, and encouragement for this formative work.

The church in a new time has much to learn from such groups. In the civic-faith era, a kind of bland and generalized friendliness seemed adequate for many. But today people seek — and formation requires — something more intentional, something with a greater depth of intimacy and honesty. A group experience where personal faith and experiences of God's presence and absence can be shared, supported, and in which people are held accountable is an ancient formative tool that is being rediscovered.

We call them "Covenant Groups" in our congregation. Some of the elements that seem crucial to their success are that groups are not self-selected gatherings of persons who are already congenial or who are "friends." When the group is made up of self-selected friends or acquaintances with whom people think they are compatible, the tendency is to lose the focus on transformation and instead become a social gathering. There is, of course, nothing wrong with social gatherings — except that that is not the purpose of these small groups. Clarity about purpose is important. We are here to support people in the process of change, of transformation to new life. It is a work that the Holy Spirit does, but with which a group of peers can assist. So our groups are intentionally mixed in the experience and background of participants. Within this broad orientation, there may be good reason at times for groups that have a particular commonality, for example, a men's group, a group for single women, or a group for young adults. Even then, however, we discourage the self-selected group as a way of helping people move beyond their comfort zone and beyond the social gathering.

Another crucial element of our groups is that they be led by trained lay leaders who are equipped for this ministry of formation and transformation. Leadership need not be heavy-handed or especially formal. Leadership tasks can be rotated among group members. But someone does need to take responsibility for keeping the group on track, focused on its purpose, and for seeing that the minimal tasks and functions necessary to group life are covered.

A third element that is crucial in these small groups is Bible study and prayer together. Depending on the congregation, this will require some training and support as well. Both biblical study and prayer are part of the formation/transformation process, ways that God the Holy Spirit can be present in our lives and our life together. We are not in this alone. Some groups also choose to participate in mission or service ministry together. They may prepare and serve a meal for homeless youth, travel together to our sister church in Nicaragua, or spend a day lobbying at the state legislature. As indicated above, these, too, can be powerfully formative experiences. In the life of a small group, they should be processed and discussed after they have taken place, explored with questions such as, "Where or how did you experience God's presence in this?"

We form our groups for a two-year period and expect a high level of commitment. At the end of two years, groups may choose to continue or to disband, allowing members to enter a new group or to take a break from the small group.

These five tools and strategies for Christian formation and delivering the goods in a new time certainly do not form an exhaustive list. There are other tools that can and should be used. In discussing these five, I have hoped to illustrate some of the ways in which the church today can be engaged in delivering the goods of a formed and transformed life in Christ as well as to provide specific illustrations and suggestions.

CHAPTER SIX

Congregational Spirituality: From Givers to Receivers Who Give

A Gathering of Givers

In the Christendom and civic-faith era, the church was often a sort of social elite. It included leaders, the "movers and shakers" in the community. There was a "Protestant establishment." This elite, sometimes defined by family and social connections, and sometimes by education and income, was not without an ethic of social responsibility. Often there was a strong — and admirable — sense of obligation: obligation to society as a whole and obligation to the less fortunate. For such an elite, with such a sense of responsibility, giving was expected and encouraged. People, often those with leadership positions and gifts, gave of themselves both in terms of money and time. Service was an important aspect of the purpose of the church in the civic-faith era.

While this was a great virtue in many ways, and one that the church today needs to continue to encourage — albeit with a greater emphasis on discipleship — there was a downside to the single-minded emphasis on and self-understanding of "givers." In fact, there were several downsides. While it may be "more blessed to give than to receive," the truth is also that it is often easier to give than to receive. Why? Giving puts a person in a position of power, which says, in effect, "I am not a person in need. You are. I have gifts, talents, skills, resources to give." To act from that position is not only to be wealthy in a certain sense, but also to be powerful.

For a number of years our congregation has had a "brother/sister church" in Managua, Nicaragua. People in Managua in general and in that church are poor — at least they are materially poor. Over the years we have sent numerous delegations of people to visit the church and the people of Nicaragua. Often we have wanted, sometimes desperately, to "do something": "Let us build houses, fix up the church, bring medical services. We have so much. Your needs are so great." And sometimes we have done such service work. But from the beginning, the pastor and the leaders of the Managua church have said: "We do not want you to come and do for us. We want you to come and be with us. We want you to know us, and we want to know you. We want to share our country, its beauties and its tragedy, with you." In other words, they did not want to have the role only of receivers, whether of material aid or assistance or skill or knowledge. And they did not allow us to behave only in the role of givers. They insisted on mutuality. They helped us to receive. Only then — and as we showed ourselves able to receive — were we also allowed to give.

In the civic-faith era, church was a place where we went to give and where we expected to give to others. Less often were we taught to receive, to see our own needs, which may not be material but are every bit as real. Not only can a one-sided emphasis on giving and behaving as giver be a power trip, but it can blind us to our own needs — for grace, for healing, for conversion, for God. Often those in civic-faith churches were encouraged to be noble by giving; but in doing so, we all implicitly discouraged the less noble part of ourselves that we all have — the part not seemingly permitted in God's presence — which was in many ways our true and our real selves. The self that is anxious and the self that is hurting; the self that is, yes, capable of giving but that also needs to receive the gifts of God and the grace of God. We need to see this self in a real and authentic way in order to share that grace with others without turning them into objects of our largess and generosity. Always or primarily to understand and present ourselves as givers, in other words, distorts our relationship with God and with our neighbors.

Learning to Be Receivers

There are countless Bible stories that help us explore this reality: that the gifted and strong are also the needy and weak in their own particular ways. There is in II Kings the wonderful story of Naaman, the Syrian general. Naaman was a great man in valor and achievement. But Naaman had a problem: he was a leper. Naaman was in need. In Naaman's story, it turns out that his need, his illness, is the source and entry to his deepest healing. His strength and military prowess are not what save him, but his need for healing — his need for the God of Israel. The Hebrew prophet Elisha brings Naaman down from his high status and power, telling him to kneel and wash himself in the "stinking ditch" of the Jordan River. As St. Paul would later discover, Naaman found out that God's grace is made perfect in weakness.

Also, in John's account of the Last Supper, we see Peter getting a lesson in receiving. When the hour finally arrives, Jesus does an unexpected thing: he strips off his clothes, wraps a towel around his waist, pours water, and prepares to wash the feet of his disciples — the work of a servant. When Jesus gets to Peter, Peter says, "No way. No, you shall not wash my feet, Lord." Peter would be fine with washing Jesus' feet, with giving, but receiving this from his Lord is just too much to bear.

Jesus answers Peter abruptly. Is this John's own version of what comes to us in the other Gospels as the famous and harsh rebuke, "Get behind me, Satan"? As reported there, Peter could not imagine Jesus suffering; and so here, it seems, Peter cannot countenance Jesus being humbled and even humiliated by washing the feet of the disciples. And Peter cannot imagine himself on the receiving end of such giving. But Jesus answers, "Unless I wash you, you have no part in me." Peter relents and allows Jesus to wash his feet — and thus learns what it is to receive. John's message probably cannot be reduced to any one point. But part of the message must be, it seems, to remind Peter and the whole church that those who would be givers must also be receivers, that those who would be instruments of God's grace for others must also receive God's grace for themselves. Apart from this, our ministry to others will be presumptuous and will rely more on self than on God and God's gifts to us.

In the civic-faith world the church was forever reminding people of their responsibilities, their obligations to others in service and action. Make no mistake, this has a place, and the church may never abandon it. However, its place is not the first place — but the second. As John puts it, "We love because God loved us first." Our giving is in response to having received.

Today I find that, as one woman said to me recently, "I do not need to be reminded, every Sunday, in each sermon, of my responsibilities. As a mother, a teacher, a wife, a church member, a citizen, my responsibilities are ever with me. What I do need to hear each week, what I need every sermon to remind me of, is God's grace." This is the first word; our response to God's grace is the second word. In this new time, it is crucial that the church get this right. Otherwise, people in congregations will find their lives distorted before God and their neighbors, and they will be without the deep experiences that fund ministry and service. Too often in the civic-faith era people were asked to bear fruit without getting their roots fed. This may have worked, in a certain sense, for elites whose roots were both fed and protected. But today the church is not a gathering of society's elite. It is, as it should be, a much more mixed gathering of haves and have-nots, of the rich and the poor and the in-betweens, especially the church in an urban setting, which is made up of a wide array of people and experiences. Alongside the stockbroker worships the man from the homeless shelter. Standing next to the teacher is the woman who experiences chronic mental illness. Indeed, the teacher herself may have experienced a debilitating clinical depression at one time in her own life. And the stockbroker may be coming to worship from his AA meeting.

We cannot assume that everyone who comes in the door is ready to be sent off on a service project. Moreover, those who do have resources and gifts also have needs — for grace, for healing, for change, for God in their lives. As one minister put it, "We used to say that 'The gospel was to comfort the afflicted and afflict the comfortable.' But in many of our churches today it is not so easy to tell who are the afflicted and who are the comfortable. We are all, in some important ways, both — both the afflicted and the comfortable."

Receiving the Sacraments

One of the ways this shift is evident in the churches I know best is in our approach to the sacraments and rituals of the church. Often those sacraments and rituals invite us into the role of receivers: "Take, eat, this bread is Christ's body, broken for you." "Take, drink, this cup is Christ's blood, shed for you."

A decade ago, at the church I serve today, the received wisdom was that "on Communion Sundays (only four Sundays a year at that time), the congregation will be half its normal size. Just accept it!" Why, I wondered, would this be the case. Certainly, anything like this is complex. But I have concluded that at least part of the reason is that, if the spiritual ethos of the congregation put a primary emphasis on giving and thus made receiving suspect, seemingly unnecessary, or even illegitimate, then the celebration of the sacrament would be diminished in significance and poorly attended. Inevitably, eating and drinking are a kind of receiving: they are a declaration that we are not full or sufficient unto ourselves. We need to be nourished, to be fed. We are hungry with a hunger the world cannot satisfy. Yet, if we are constantly or solely being described as givers and doers, those who must build the kingdom, what place is there in our faith for receiving, for acknowledging our need, for the grace that is conveyed by the sacrament?

Today, in that same congregation, the worship attendance on those Sundays when Communion is celebrated (now seven rather than four times a year) is if anything higher than on other Sundays. Why? Again, the reasons are complex. There has been education, in multiple settings, about the sacraments, both Baptism and the Lord's Supper. The ways in which communion is celebrated now include not only receiving the elements in the pews (the traditional style of Reformed churches) but also coming forward to receive the elements from a pastor or deacon. But beneath and around all this is the fact that permission has been given for congregants to be receivers, to acknowledge our need for grace and nourishment, and for Christ's ministry to us, as well as through us.

Today also this congregation has a regular Sunday each year for the renewal of baptismal vows and covenants. As part of this service, those baptized persons who wish are invited to come forward to a pastor who will take water from the baptismal font, touch it to their forehead, and say, "Remember your baptism and be thankful." "Remember your baptism" may mean "recall the actual experience," but it also means "Remember that by the grace of God — not because you are so good but because God is so good — you are a child of God, a disciple of Christ and a member of the church. This is God's gift to you and to us all, our identity in Christ as baptized and beloved children of the Most High God. Because this is God's doing, we say, it cannot be taken from you."

People, from the first, have responded eagerly to this powerful reminder of God's grace and love. Indeed, baptism itself has been reclaimed, first of all, as God's doing and God's grace, God's singular gift that names us and defines our identity. In baptism and its renewal, we are receivers.

From Obligation to Motivation

This shift from "givers" to "receivers who give" has had other implications and ways that it has expressed itself in the congregation and in the spirituality of the congregation. One of these implications is a corollary shift from obligation to motivation. In the civic-faith era, "church going" was often experienced and described in the language of obligation. It was something one was expected to do as a member of the community, as a good citizen and a decent and responsible person. For better or worse, few people, especially in the secular Pacific Northwest, feel any obligation to attend or participate in the church anymore. Obligation is more likely to be felt toward family or self-care, leading to family activities and sports on Sundays. On the plus side of the ledger, people are more likely to seek and participate in church today because they are motivated to do so. They are motivated by their need for depth in their lives, by their need for God, their need for meaning, or their need for community. They may come because they need forgiveness and the healing of their spirits. The church that will speak to a society where people no longer come solely or primarily out of a sense of obligation, but because they are motivated to do so, will be a church that maintains a balanced spirituality of giving and receiving.

Leaders Who Are Led

This shift is also expressed in how leaders understand themselves and their leadership role, whether as leaders in the congregation or the wider community. There was a time when those who became leaders in the church were chosen for that role because they were leaders in secular society. They had the bearing, the history, the connections, and perhaps the skills to lead in church as well. Today I find that people are more often called to leadership in the church because of their own faith and faith experience. They are grounded, and they are mature Christians. They are people of faith. This does not mean that they are without needs, or that they are perfect. Quite the contrary, it may mean that they know well — and are able to share — their own needs and imperfections.

Another way to put this would be to say that, in congregations where the shift in congregational spirituality from "givers" to "receivers who give" has been experienced and supported, the leaders are those who are also led. They seek and respond to the leading of God, of Christ, and of the Holy Spirit in their lives. They are not solo operators. They recognize that being a leader involves an openness to and a capacity for the Spirit. As leaders they are learning to say, and to mean, "Not my will, but thy will be done." Their leadership is funded by worship experience, by prayer, and by study of the Scriptures. Simply being a leader or leadership type in the community or in secular society does not always translate to leadership in the church.

There was a time in the civic-faith culture and church where one could be a leader, or a key member of the church board, without regularly participating in the worship life of the congregation. There was a way in which particular boards, often those having to do with finances, were made up of "heavy-hitters," "old money family members," and the "well-connected." And being one of these was sufficient basis for such a role or position in the church of the civic-faith era. Today — in a congregation where leadership is connected to one's faith and experience of God — it is rare to see people in leadership positions for such reasons as being "connected" or representing "old money." Leaders are those who are led — led by the Spirit. They are givers who have received.

CHAPTER SEVEN

From Board Culture to Ministry Culture

In the era of American Christendom, "mission" came to be thought of, in many ways, as something that occurred beyond the borders of America. So closely identified were Western culture and the Christian faith that there was a tendency to think of the mission field as "over there," "overseas" — focused on non-Western and "foreign" peoples and lands. During the nineteenth century, particularly, a host of mission organizations and efforts sprang up that directed the attention and resources of American congregations to the "foreign mission field."

There were a number of difficulties with this identification of Western and American culture with the Christian faith and the gospel, not least being that the capacity for a gospel critique of Western culture was severely diminished. In addition, when the mission field was thought to be overseas, when mission began at the border of the Christian empire, and Western society and Christianity were more or less synonymous, it meant that there was no mission at home. At home there were efforts to ameliorate the suffering brought on by industrialization, and the church did exercise a role as the conscience of the community and society; but it was — or was thought to be — a Christian society, in which most everyone was some sort of Christian.

With this framework at work, the job of church members was not to be engaged in mission or ministry themselves; they were to maintain the parish. Moreover, the primary way in which to maintain the parish, to participate in the church, was to serve on the growing structure of church boards and committees. In other words, and as Tom Bandy has argued, people were asked to be engaged in the *management* of ministry and of the church rather than in ministry or mission themselves. With maintaining and enhancing the life of the parish as the focus, "mission" often came to be thought of as simply one of the many things a congregation did. It was a part of the budget, an activity of a committee, the sending of money to the denomination for the real work of mission, in far-off lands and distant exotic cultures.

But today the new post-Christendom, postmodern era is upon us, and the church is once again seeing that "mission" is not a department, a budget, the activity of a designated "mission" committee or the transfer of resources overseas. In this new time, everything the church does is, in some sense, mission. In our secular, religiously pluralistic, Western context, every congregation is — at least potentially — a mission outpost, a beachhead of the empire of God in the midst of the empire of America. "Mission" is not one of the many programs of the church; the church exists for mission, for the changing and transforming of human beings and human communities, in light of the gospel.

A somewhat different way to put this is to say that the mission field has moved. No longer is it overseas or in distant, non-Western cultures — it is closer to home. In fact, it is at the doorstep or our churches. Indeed, it is inside our sanctuaries as we engage there in the work of changing, healing, and transforming, and of sorting out gospel values from Western culture and its values. Mission no longer belongs to the "missionary" working in tandem with the soldier of the empire. (One of the reasons that "mission" may be a lost word for churches is that it came to be associated with a certain cultural imperialism.) But today's mission and ministry are in our Western society, in the neighborhoods of our congregations, and in the sanctuaries of our churches.

This is the backdrop for the shift from "board culture to ministry culture." The work that was asked of congregation members in earlier times, participating in running the church, has been changed in this new time to a calling of congregation members to be engaged in ministry themselves, not simply to manage the church's ministry and the clergy's ministry. During the Christendom era, when people got involved in running the church here, and mission was relegated to distant lands, there were two further downsides to the formulation. One was that too often the church, rather than sending people into the world in ministry, tied people up in the administration and activities of the church. And when congregations became inward focused and inward looking, the interaction with the culture at large was reduced.

The congregation I serve has a lovely egg-shaped sanctuary. People come into this oval sanctuary by walking through a sort of hall-like entryway that resembles nothing so much as a birth canal. The hall-like entry has a low ceiling, but as you step into the sanctuary, it opens up to a large womb-like place. Worship, at least in part, involves regression. We return to the womb, to the source — and to something larger than ourselves. We are permitted a legitimate dependence. In worship we seek to regain perspective, the perspective provided by our faith and by our relationship with God. But we are not permitted to stay there, to remain perpetually dependent. At the conclusion of the service, with the benediction, we are sent out — rebirthed into the world. We are thrust out of the birth canal, out of the womb for another week, to live as Christ's apostles — thrust out as those who are sent. When we confuse mission with getting everybody involved on committees, task forces, and boards within the congregation, we tend to get people stuck in the church. We tend to confuse ministry of the laity with running the church. In reality, the primary ministry of the laity is to represent Christ to the world.

A second drawback to the board culture is that it tends to create — or at least reinforce — a notion of first- and second-class Christians and church members. The first-class Christians are those at the center of the church's organizational life. Often in congregations I have heard people say, "Unless you are on a board you aren't really part of things at the church." So congregations tend to have one group of people who are active on boards and another, often larger, group who are "not active" or not as active. In this framework, the way you experience a sense of belonging is by being involved in church governance and management. Because there are, typically, a limited number of offices and board slots, only a portion of the congregation then experiences this sense of belonging, of being a part of things.

If, on the other hand, being a Christian is not mainly about managing the church but about ministry, then such levels and circles need not exist. All Christians can be involved in ministry. For some, their daily occupations will be the primary arena of ministry; for others, it will be their vocation as parents; others will take part in ministries that call forth their particular gifts. None of this should be taken to mean that congregations do not require effective governance and administration. They certainly do: good governance and effective administration are important and necessary. Those individuals who have and use such gifts within the congregation, whether as staff members or volunteers, are a great asset to any church. This is, however, but one form of ministry. Many congregations can reduce the structures of governance and administration, thus freeing people for other forms of ministry and redefining the ministry of the laity so that we do not think of it primarily as managing the church.

One congregation I know has reduced its official board structure to three boards, which is the minimum complement required by denominational polity. But alongside the three boards are sixty-three "ministry teams." Some are focused on ministries within the church, e.g., worship planning. Others are focused beyond the congregation, building homes for the poor and justice advocacy for migrants. The point of the structure is that most people in the congregation are not asked to "run the church." They are invited and encouraged to be involved in ministry, serving the needs of others, sharing faith, and bringing about change and transformation in human beings.

My own congregation is in the process of such a shift from board culture to ministry culture. Because it has been my observation that people more readily let go of the old when they can see the new, we are encouraging and developing ministry teams, which I will discuss in more detail below. As ministry teams take hold and people participate through them, our structure of boards and committees will be reduced. People will shift from the management of ministry to actually doing ministry.

The Shift from Board Culture to Ministry Culture

If the first part of this chapter has succeeded in providing the need and framework for the shift from board culture to ministry culture, then the question is, How? How do persons and congregations make the shift? What is necessary to make the rhetoric real? Three elements seem crucial: the cycle of transformation, identifying and affirming gifts and callings, and equipping and training persons for ministry.

No one should imagine that the shift from board culture to ministry culture means less work. It requires significant work; but it is different work. Instead of getting people into the circle of those who are "active in the church," it is about engaging people in the cycle of transformation. Instead of the often elaborate process of nominations, it is about identifying and affirming gifts for ministry. Instead of board training and retreats, it is about equipping and training people for ministry. But let me repeat that this shift does not mean that the church can wholly dispense with boards or faithful and effective administration. It cannot. Congregations that are operated and administered by one person or one small group — without accountability — are systems asking for trouble. Good governance and administration remain important, but they represent work that is required of a relative (and accountable) few rather than many.

The Cycle of Transformation

Earlier I mentioned how worship is a kind of return to the womb. We regress, lean upon the everlasting arms, rest in the bosom of Abraham, and experience a legitimate dependence. But we must not remain there. Our experience of dependence allows us to stand again on our own two feet, to go forth into the world as ministers and apostles. Another way to put this is to say that the worship, the teaching and learning, and the fellowship life of the church transforms us, week by week, and throughout a lifetime, from disciples to apostles. Disciples are followers — students — of a teacher. Apostles are those who are themselves sent out by the teacher to teach. During the time of Jesus' ministry, his disciples followed him, listened to him, watched him. Occasionally, they were themselves sent out. The book of Acts tells the story of how those who were once disciples got a new name, job title, and position description. No longer were they disciples; now they were apostles and ministers, sent into the world with the gift of the Holy Spirit, to act and teach as Jesus had done. Too often the church has allowed people to stay at the listening, watching, and learning stage of things, and has not made the move to send them out to become teachers, actors, and ministers themselves. Or to put it another way, people have been the *objects* of mission and ministry without becoming the *subjects* of mission and ministry.

This church works at this transformation through worship, faith development (or teaching and learning), and through fellowship in Christian community. In order for people to be changed, to be called to ministry, each of these must be in place and vital.

The first and most important is powerful worship, which I focused on in chapter three. The crucial point is that worship is not an informational event. It is not a time to inform people about the church; it is not a time to inform people about the Christian faith; and it is not a time to inform people about God. It is a time to experience God, to experience the sacred, in ways that are life-changing. Too often worship in the mainline churches is an informational event rather than a formational and transformational event. But if information were all that was needed to save us, we would have been redeemed long ago. For the most part, we do not need more information. We need God. Worship is the encounter with God: it is "meeting" — and being met by — the Holy One.

In the Christendom era, and in many mainline churches today, worship is nice but is not absolutely necessary, not critical. Thus in the typical mainline congregation the average attendance at worship represents about 30-40 percent of the congregation's membership. In our new time, worship will be experienced as essential, not something you can miss. Congregations that are involved in the cycle of transformation need to aim for a much higher percentage of their membership (perhaps 80 percent) in worship every Sunday.

The faith development, or teaching and learning ministries, of the congregation are also crucial to the cycle of transformation, as people move weekly — and throughout a lifetime — from disciples to apostles. Once again, it is important to underscore that teaching and learning are not primarily or exclusively focused on the young. Too many congregations offer worship for adults and education for children, and they are perplexed when young people grow up and leave the church, often seeming to experience confirmation as graduation! But as Clarence Jordan reminds us, "You can't raise live chicks under dead hens!" If we want God to touch the lives of the young children and youths in our churches, then the lives of adults will need to be touched and changed. The congregation itself, not the Sunday school, is the primary formative experience for the young. Just as we need to expect 80 percent of the congregation to regularly participate in worship, we need to expect 80 percent of the congregation to be involved in some experience of faith development — whether through classes, small groups, or through mentors teaching others.

In addition to worship and teaching and learning, fellowship is a key part of the cycle of transformation of disciples into apostles. "Fellowship" has become a very tepid word in the church, what some identify as the primary sacrament of the Protestant church — the coffee or fellowship hour after the worship service. I have nothing against the coffee hour (after all, I live in Seattle), but fellowship is more than this. Christian fellowship is gathering with others who are engaged in the cycle of transformation, who are being changed, and who are being formed in a Christian spiritual life. For many, the coffee hour needs to be, if not replaced, then supplemented by a smaller group that focuses on developing significant and intimate relationships with others who seek to have a spiritual life and relationship with God. For many, part of that cycle of transformation will be regular participation in such a group for prayer, Bible study, support, and accountability in Christian life and ministry.

These are the key elements of the cycle of transformation: powerful worship, faith development through teaching and learning ministries, and authentic Christian fellowship. In one important sense, each of these is an end and not merely a means. But they are also — and at the same time — a means to Christian formation, to helping people continually move through the process of disciples becoming apostles. But at some point, often earlier than we think, there is no substitute for action, for just trying it and doing it. I remember my first internship as a seminary student. I didn't know much — maybe nothing. Yet I was entrusted with the leadership of a small group for prayer, Bible study, and spiritual friendship. I was being pushed out of the nest, asked to do and to lead; and in the process I learned.

I recall another experience that happened at about the same time. A man who was drunk showed up at the church asking for help. I was the only one there, so it was impossible to refer him to someone else. I had to respond, somehow, to him. This led to a memorable six-block walk to a hospital de-tox facility. This wasn't so much a walk together, given his falling-down condition, as it was an embrace — a clumsy dance. As he desperately held onto me, I realized that I had never been that close to a drunk before. I had never felt what it was like to be in the clutches of someone who was "making a scene," and to be viewed by those who hurried by as part of the scene — possibly a troublemaker myself. In its way, it was quite liberating to be in that spot!

Too often in the church we have the idea that people cannot get involved in ministry until they are fully trained, equipped, certified, graduated, and ordained. Nonsense! There is no evidence that God delayed until Moses got his act together, or that Peter was chosen because his record was impeccable, or that Paul fully understood where God was leading before he got engaged in the great work. Part of the learning cycle, the cycle of transformation, is on-the-job training. Having said that, however, I must emphasize that there is still a place for the discernment of gifts and for equipping people for their ministries, which are vital parts of making the shift from a board culture to a ministry culture.

The Ministry of All God's People

In the Christendom era, and in a board culture, the question congregational leaders often asked was, "How can we get the needs of the church as institution met?" "How can we fill the slots on the Nominating Committee report?" "How can we get people to serve on the various boards and committees that the church requires in order to function?" The perspective behind all such questions is, "How can individuals be enlisted to serve the needs of the institution?"

A different perspective is suggested by taking "gifts for ministry" as the starting point. The question then becomes not how we can enlist individuals to serve the institution, but how the institution (or congregation), through its life and ministry, can help people identify, claim, and exercise their gifts for ministry. Doing this work is a ministry that the church offers to people as a part of the process and cycle of transformation. So instead of the annual effort to fill the slots on the Nominating Committee's report, the congregation that is moving from board culture to ministry culture will see the work of helping people to identify, claim, and exercise their gifts as part of the ongoing work of Christian formation. It is as integral to a congregation's life as worship or faith development.

Not only will the congregation that has embraced the ministry culture approach see itself as helping people identify, claim, and exercise the gifts for ministry that God has given them, but that congregation will help people make the link between their gifts and appropriate forms of service and witness. The name our church uses to identify this work is "The Ministry of All God's People." It has several elements. One is the effort to help people identify their own gifts for ministry. A number of useful "gifts inventory" formats are available, and some congregations have created their own. These may be used as people become new members of the congregation. But it may also make sense to use these only after people, especially those who are new Christians, have spent some time immersed in the life of worship, faith development, and fellowship.

A complementary, second element of the Ministry of All God's People is what we call "ministry mentors." These are lay members of the congregation who are equipped to help people identify their gifts and then link them to ministries of the congregation that will give them an opportunity to do ministry. For some it may be a group working in "Creation Care"; for others working at a residential spiritual community for those experiencing mental illness. Others will be called to teach in the Sunday school or sing in a choir. Still others will come to understand their own vocation as the primary arena in which they exercise their gifts for ministry.

As part of this work of the "ministry mentors" and the linking of people and their gifts to opportunities for service and witness, our congregation makes a special effort to identify ministry opportunities that are intergenerational as well as those that parents can do with their children. The research work by the Search Institute on the faith development of children clearly indicates that a crucial childhood experience is participating in service and action projects and ministries with their parents or other adults.

A third element of our Ministry of All God's People, in addition to "gifts inventories" and "ministry mentors," is the "ministry team." In every congregation, some people will discern a call to a form of ministry that may not already exist in that congregation's life. So long as that ministry is within a broad definition of the congregation's goals, a ministry team approach says, "Let's run this one up the flagpole and see if others believe themselves called to joined you." If so, the congregation and its leaders charter a new ministry team, help to provide training and resources, and say, "Go and do ministry, and keep us posted."

The "keep us posted" approach is in marked contrast to the norm in the usual board culture settings. Instead of giving people permission and encouragement to respond to God's call, the board culture congregations and their leaders are likely to say, "We will look into that and we'll keep you posted." This has two unhappy effects: first, it tends to discourage people who want to do ministry; second, it tends to overload clergy and other church leaders. Instead of everything being done by congregational leaders or having to receive authorization from a board, with the resulting "We'll look into that and keep you posted," a ministry culture approach says, "Go and do ministry, and you keep us posted."

This is a way of "giving responsibility back," which empowers members of a congregation and keeps its leaders from collapsing under the burden of expectations. Long ago I learned to respond to those who eagerly articulated a view about "what the church should do" by saying, "I am not able to help you if what you want is for others (the church) to do this ministry. But I am very much interested in helping you discern your own calling and gifts for ministry, and in exercising those." Another way to put this is to say that in a board culture members of congregations often assume a passive role as "consumers of ministry." Ministry is something done for others, a kind of product or service provided by "ministers," by ordained clergy and a relatively small group of lay leaders. In this understanding, people go to church to consume the ministry products generated by others. What's lost in such a consumer-oriented approach to the church is the whole conviction and experience of the priesthood of all believers. Ministry is not a product or service generated by some for others in the congregation to consume; it is a way of life and living in which all are invited to share.

A fourth element of our Ministry of All God's People is training people for ministry and equipping them with the resources they need. In many ways, the cycle of transformation described above is the basic training of people for ministry. Beyond that, persons engaged in particular forms of ministry may require additional information, skills, or training. In some cases these are available within the congregation, either from its clergy or laity. In other instances, congregations may send people for appropriate training or bring people in who can provide this training. As an example, let me briefly cite a ministry that we call "special friends" — persons in the congregation who are paired with adults who are frail, elderly, or in some other way limited. The "special friends" visit their person on a regular basis. Some read to their special friend; some assist them in getting to a doctor; some help them with troubleshooting; some simply listen. And some pray with their special friends. At least once a year, and sometimes more often, a training event is held for the thirty-five or so people who participate in this ministry as "special friends." Usually a specialist in aging provides a workshop in which special friends have the opportunity to reflect on their ministries, to learn new skills and information, and to become aware of resources they may use.

Our church does another kind of training with those who will work in some area of our mental health ministry, or in legislative advocacy, or who will travel to third-world countries to work among congregations there. The nature and extent of training depends on the ministry people are embarking on or in which they are engaged.

The fifth and final element of the Ministry of All God's People is encouraging people to reflect on their experiences of ministry and what they have learned about themselves, others, and their faith. If people have spent a week together building homes with Habitat for Humanity, it is important to gather such a group and invite them to reflect on how they experienced God's presence in that work. If people have been engaged in an effort to thwart gambling in their community or in the legislature, it is important that the group gather to reflect on their ministry, to pray together, and to seek the guidance of the Holy Spirit. If some have been called to a ministry of working with the victims of gun violence, they too need occasions for support and accountability in these ministries.

A colleague of mine has suggested three useful questions to guide reflection on such a practice of ministry: What did I give? What did I receive? Where did I encounter God? These questions not only provide a simple format for reflection, they also help to affirm the two sides of this ministry — both giving and receiving — and to transcend the too-simple dichotomy of "in-reach" and "outreach." I offer our "Ministry of All God's People" experience not as normative, but as illustrative.

The crucial point is to generate and operate from expectations born of a ministry culture. A ministry culture approach believes and expects that all people have been given gifts for ministry. Moreover, it believes that ministry belongs to the church as a whole; it does not belong to the ordained alone. The Reformers had it right: baptism is our ordination to ministry. This new time in the post-Christendom era makes it possible for the church to reappropriate the Reformers' insight in a new way. The ministry of the laity is to represent Christ to and in the world; the ministry of the ordained is to equip the saints for ministry.

Finally, one might observe that the board culture tends to operate from a scarcity approach: "There are all these board slots, positions, offices — how will we ever fill them?" A ministry culture tends to operate from the idea of abundance: God gives all people gifts for ministry. The church's task is to help people discover, identify, claim, and exercise those gifts. In that way we will get as much "ministry" done as God calls forth.

CHAPTER EIGHT

From Community Organization to Faith-Based Ministry

Paul Sherry, immediate past president of the United Church of Christ, was once invited to speak at the dedication of a new youth center in Chicago. At the time, Sherry was the executive director of the Chicago Renewal Society, a social-service agency that had Christian roots. Another one of the speakers was Harold Washington, then mayor of Chicago, who had had many associations with Sherry. After the ceremony, Mayor Washington invited Sherry to have a cup of coffee with him at a local diner. When they sat down, Mayor Washington quickly got to the reason for the invitation:

"You know, Paul, I appreciate all of your efforts in getting this center opened, and I also appreciated your remarks today. But you are a Christian minister and I didn't hear you say anything today that couldn't have been said by somebody else. We need to hear something else from you. We need to hear something from the gospel!"

It is no coincidence that this reminder came from an African-American to a European-American. African-American Christians have had more than ample reminders that the language of the oppressive host culture is not enough to sustain social action. Something else is required; that something else is called the gospel. I don't tell this story to sit in judgment on one of my own denomination's leaders, because it might have happened to many of us mainline church leaders who had learned the habits of Christendom. Our social witness was often secularized beyond recognition. Much of what we did under the rubrics of "mission," or "social outreach and action," became indistinguishable from that of many another community organization dedicated to social betterment.

As I have suggested in the preceding chapter, during the Christendom era we came to see mission as something that happened beyond the borders of the nation and culture. At home we lived in a Christian society. So we dropped or minimized the particular language and grounding of the Christian faith community as we went about such work. Many of our social service and action efforts were no different in grounding or language from countless other similar efforts and programs that had no faith basis or church connection. The social service of the church became secularized. Its work in this area often became a matter of supporting a host of community organizations or being another community organized with historic ties to the church and Christian faith.

Similarly, programs and institutions that began in the church and had roots in the Christian faith lost their capacity to speak their mother tongue. Recently, while my daughter and I were driving in downtown Seattle, we passed the downtown YMCA, and she asked me, "What does YMCA stand for?"

"It stands for Young Men's Christian Association," I said.

"Really?" she responded, clearly surprised. "I thought it was an exercise place!" Not only YMCAs and YWCAs, but colleges, universities, hospitals, and service agencies have gradually let go of their faith identity to become secularized programs concerned with social service and betterment.

Meanwhile, in the life of local congregations, "mission" often meant that the congregation would allocate money to support a host of such community organizations, which we understood to be doing, in some very broad sense, "the work of the church." These might include, for example, a shelter for the homeless, a drug-addiction treatment program, a coalition working to ban handguns, a public-school reform effort, a legal-aid clinic, a meals-on-wheels program for the elderly, or any number of similar community organizations. Obviously, there is nothing wrong with any of these efforts in themselves. They may be doing very significant work. The problematic part is that, in thinking of our society as in some sense Christian, we assumed it was enough to "do good" without rooting such work in faith and connecting it to the Body of Christ. In fact, on more than one occasion it was perceived that an obvious connection to the church might be a liability! Moreover, this has proven problematic because "mission," rather than being understood as intrinsic to the life of the church, became a particular program, department, or budget item. "Mission" was one of the many varied activities of a church, not its core.

The new times in which we live offer the opportunity to move from mission as supporting or even being another community organization to a more fully, and unapologetic, faith-based ministry. There are two crucial reasons that the evolution of church mission into supporting various community organizations has proven problematic in the new post-Christendom era in which we find ourselves. But the flip side of each of these problems reveals opportunities for our present age.

One reason that the tendency of the church to secularize its mission and to support a host of community organizations is problematic is that we began to think of "mission" primarily as simply sending money. Congregations had "mission budgets"; we strove to send a certain percentage of our overall budget to our denomination for "mission." We enacted elaborate formulas to ensure that for every dollar spent "on ourselves," a certain amount was spent "on others." (Of course, such a dichotomy already signals problems! It suggests that we have come to think of the church as "ours," or "our club.") Still, most of this represented good-faith efforts toward sharing and doing what was seen to be appropriate.

But Christian mission, while never less than sharing and sending money, is always more than that. What was lost in reducing mission to sending money and to supporting a variety of community groups and causes was the twofold opportunity to practice discipleship and to be in relationship with those whom we would serve. In our congregation we have not abandoned our support of various community and denominational agencies and programs; but alongside those we have developed what we call "Major Mission Projects." These are ministries of the congregation, funded by the church, but which provide, among other things, opportunities for people in the congregation to practice discipleship. They may work as interns in a job-training center with our brother-sister church in Nicaragua. They may be part of the resident or volunteer staff at a residential spiritual community for those suffering from mental illness. Or they may work alongside members of a new congregation that our church is sponsoring — as that new church takes shape. Each of these "Major Mission" projects is clearly a ministry of the church and one that offers people in the church the opportunity to practice discipleship. This does not replace sending or allocating money; but in addition to sending money, we send human beings.

Part of practicing and experiencing discipleship in this way is the experience of being with those who are suffering and in some way excluded from society. Jesus frequently reminds us that the suffering and the marginalized will often prove to be our teachers in the faith. Such has been the case. Sometimes the lessons are difficult — something like the slap of the Zen master. I recall, for example, the story of the young woman who worked hard to prepare a magnificent soup for homeless men. When she set a steaming bowl down in front of her first aid recipient and then lingered in the hope of an acknowledgment and expression of gratitude, the man finally looked up and said, "Doing good's a hustle too!"

Other times the lesson is a gentler one. Whenever members of our congregation spend time with people at our partner church in Nicaragua, they return marveling at the generosity of the poor. "How is it," we wonder, "that those who have so little can be so generous?" It is, of course, a lesson that Jesus himself pointed out on more than one occasion. On other occasions, as we work alongside those who are struggling to free themselves of addictions, we come to see and understand our own addictions and our own fears. Time and again, people who commit themselves to the practice of discipleship and to work among the suffering and the excluded report that they went to give, but found that they received much more than they gave. In such experiences we begin to realize that mission and ministry are not the beneficent gesture of those who have much toward those who have little, because we freely recognize how much we have to gain.

As we move from the idea of mission as the church sending money for an activity carried on by community organizations to the concept of faith-based ministries, we rediscover our own need to practice discipleship and how formative such experience is for faith.

A second reason for the inadequacy of turning mission into support of community organizations — and thus forgetting or marginalizing the faith basis — is that so many of our most intractable social problems have a spiritual element or dimension. They often prove to be, at their core, spiritual problems that involve people's deepest selves and their worldviews, as well as society's principalities and powers. In providing low-income housing, for example, our congregation has gradually come to the realization that many of those who are homeless need much more than a roof over their heads. A place to sleep is a start; but often much more than this is required if people are to heal and become whole. They need relationships in which they begin to experience love. Like all the rest of us who would detoxify from a culture that is toxic in its materialism, individualism, and violence, they need a whole new life — new attitudes, new relationships, new practices, new perspectives. They need God.

To bracket faith out, as often happens in secularized community organizations, is to bracket out the issues that may be at the very heart of healing and new life. This is not to say that, in the shift from community organizations to more faith-based ministries, we use material aid and other forms of assistance as a way of inducing religious faith or conformity. A faith that is not freely chosen is not faith and will not lead to enduring change. A faith that is manipulated in others or extorted from them does not witness to or affirm Christ. It denies him. But our choice is not between force-feeding faith or being mum about it. The point is to learn how to share our own faith and experience of God with others and to receive their sharing of their faith and experience of God with us.

In many ways, Alcoholics Anonymous and similar "twelve-step" programs provide a model of faith-based ministry. At the heart of AA is the recognition that dealing with an addiction is a spiritual matter, one that requires facing one's deepest fears, longings, and pain, and seeking a relationship with a power not our own. But in AA at its best there are no experts, only fellow travelers on the journey. AA provides a kind of model for faith-based ministry that recognizes that many problems go beyond material aid, and it engages people at a spiritual level. Healing requires a turning in one's life. It requires honesty with oneself and others; it means support and accountability in community; it means new practices, new ways of living. It means surrender.

When Harold Washington asked Paul Sherry for "the gospel," he was asking for this. Not religious arrogance, but not religious reticence either. Instead, a recognition that the church serves the world best when the church is true to itself, when it is the church.

In making this shift, our congregation has moved from "mission" understood primarily as funding a host of agencies and programs for social betterment to mission as being involved in God's healing work in the world. This has meant the move toward faith-based ministries in which people practice discipleship, give to and receive from the suffering and the excluded, and address the needs of the world as people rooted in a life-changing faith. Organizationally, this shift has taken form in two ways. First, "Ministry Teams" (discussed above), whose basic idea is that everyone in the church is called to ministry (rather than managing the church). Part of what goes on in the life of the church is helping people discern their calling, claim their gifts for ministry, and link with opportunities to be in ministry. Some will be focused within the congregation's ministries of worship, teaching, and fellowship. Others will focus primarily on service and witness in the larger community. Rather than determining ministry areas from the top down, ministry teams invite people to respond to the hopes and hurts that move and call to them.

A somewhat more complex version of a similar impulse we have named "Major Mission Projects." Like the ministry teams, Major Mission Projects are not top down but bottom up. People within the congregation are encouraged and helped to discern a call, to formulate a ministry, to work with a group that does have gifts for planning and administration to shape the ministry, and then to seek the support of the congregation for this venture. Typically, ministry teams' budgets are modest or none. Major Mission Projects, on the other hand, have significant budgets. The three Major Missions currently ongoing (Plymouth House of Healing, a residential, spiritual community for persons with mental illness; The Alice Hooker Women's Job Training and Vocational Center in Managua, Nicaragua; and Bethany United Church of Christ, a multiracial, multicultural, new church start) have annual budgets of $30,000 to $50,000.

While we seek to maintain the "permission giving" spirit of a ministry team approach, we have developed a series of criteria for the Major Mission projects. These are intended not only as a way of sorting among ideas and proposals, but to help those with a vision to focus and direct their energies. The seven criteria used to evaluate a Major Mission project proposal are the following:

1. A ministry to which we believe God is calling Plymouth Church.
2. A ministry that is clearly related to Plymouth Church and identifiable as a ministry of the church.

3. A ministry that provides varied opportunities for service and participation by Plymouth members and friends, including opportunities for intergenerational participation.
4. A ministry that uses the resources of the congregation wisely for significant impact.
5. A ministry that is timely in meeting a current or emerging need by responding to specific human hurts and hopes, by responding to voices from the community of need, by responding with a willingness to risk, even seeking to do "the impossible."
6. A ministry that many in the congregation find exciting, inspiring, and an effort they want to support.
7. A ministry that is viable, fundable, sustainable, and likely to meet stated goals.

Again, I offer this example as illustrative rather than prescriptive. My point is not that other congregations should adopt this particular model, but it is to share one possible approach to moving from mission as support of or being another community organization to mission as faith-based ministry.

Among the criteria, my personal favorite is found in number five: ". . . even seeking to do the impossible." At many points in these ventures we have found ourselves attempting to do "the impossible." At least, impossible for us. This proves, for mainline Protestants, a good place to be. When we attempt what is not possible for us, we learn what it means to turn to God, to rely on God, to move from self-reliance to faith. In such moments and experiences, our attempts at faith-based ministry become not only an attempt to act from out of our faith and to share it. They prove to be powerful and profound formative faith experiences in themselves.

I remember the day I encountered a member of the group working on developing the Plymouth House of Healing. The night before, the group had interviewed three applicants for a leadership position on the staff. "Which one did you hire?" I asked. "Well, you know," she said, "we didn't hire any of them. After the interviews we felt the need to go back to the drawing board. We felt the need for prayer and discernment. We weren't ready to make a decision." I knew that this particular faith-based ministry really would be faith-based!

CHAPTER NINE

From Democracy to Discernment

After reading the earlier chapter entitled "From Board Culture to Ministry Culture," some readers may conclude that I view boards as a lost cause or a bad thing. It's true that I believe we have, in the Christendom era, confused managing the church with ministry, or the primary ministry of the laity, and thus encouraged far too many people to be engaged in church management. Rather than equipping people for the ministry of the laity — representing Christ to the world — the tendency has been to equip them to run the church. In the Christendom era, when we believed that we lived in a Christian society and the mission field was overseas, this made a certain kind of sense. But this is no longer the case.

Our goal in this new time, when the mission field is all around us, is to help people be engaged in ministry. Still, congregational governance remains important. Boards and committees, perhaps in more limited number, have a place. Congregational and denominational gatherings and meetings for decision-making will continue to be necessary and important, even if they are not as central in the experience of people's engagement in the church and in their faith. But here, too, the new era in which we find ourselves invites and requires a shift — a shift from democracy to discernment.

As I pointed out in the preceding chapter, during the Christendom and modern eras there was a frequently uncritical and sometimes tragic identification of Western culture with Christianity. The two marched arm in arm into non-Western cultures and lands, suggesting by their close alliance that to embrace Western culture and its norms was to embrace Christianity, and vice versa. Of course, in a time when in the U.S. being a good Christian was not particularly different from being a responsible citizen, it would make sense that as Christianity encountered other cultures and faiths around the world, Western culture and values were all wrapped up with the Christian faith. One of the opportunities and necessities of our new age is to unwrap that package and for Western Christians to become as discerning about their own culture and its biases as they are about any other.

Given this close and often assumed identification of Western culture with Christian faith, the church was often secularized. Just as being a good Christian was not all that different from being a good citizen, so being the church was not all that different from being another civic institution in Western society. Thus meetings in the church, congregational meetings, and denominational meetings often came to look and operate more like democracy and democratic decision-making than Christian discernment. Over and over, it seems, we have experienced a strange bifurcation. Generally such meetings begin with prayer; sometimes, at denominational assemblies, there will be a half hour or so devoted to Bible study. Then the meeting itself will begin, and there will be no relationship whatsoever between the meeting and the prayer and biblical study that began the day! We put on our church hats for half an hour — singing, praying, and studying the Bible. Then we take them off and put on our citizen hats as we proceed to the business at hand.

In this way we have often promoted and supported a false distinction between "spiritual life" and "business life." It is a distinction we would deny in theory; but it often prevails in practice. One is often hard put to see the connection between the 11:00 worship service and the congregational meeting that follows at noon.

My colleague Martin Copenhaver, in some research and writing on our own denominational heritage (Congregational), has concluded that early Congregationalists may have practiced something that looked, to the uninformed, like democracy, but was different. It is better described as "discernment." What is the difference?

"The early Congregationalists believed that the workings of the Holy Spirit can be discerned in community by receptive hearts that are informed by scripture and molded in prayer. They put into practice their understanding that the gathered community is the true vessel of the Spirit of Christ — a term that they used often. They met often, and their meetings were seen as opportunities to encounter God in their midst. That is, they were more like worship than legislative sessions. The community did not gather for decision-making as much as discernment. They listened to one another, not out of a humanist notion that people of an opposing view are worthy of respect, but because one can never know whom the Spirit will choose to speak through on any given occasion."

Of course, this is not the heritage of every congregation. Nevertheless, the understanding is available to us all. When we meet as church, we depend on the Holy Spirit. Moreover, the conviction that we listen to others respectfully not because we believe "everyone is entitled to their opinion" but because one never knows whom the Spirit will speak through — this is an idea that can help all congregations move from democracy to discernment.

"A 'majority rules' way of thinking," observes Copenhaver, "is what happens when we take God out of the congregational process. It is not that *no one* can tell us what to do (a frequent claim of American Christians, especially those in churches with a congregational polity). Rather, we seek together to discern what *Christ* would have us do. We listen to one another because we are listening for the voice of the Spirit, and you never know whom the Spirit will choose to speak through. We wait upon the Spirit, as did the people of Pentecost, the Spirit that alone is able to fashion understanding and unity out of diversity."

Especially for congregations in the free-church tradition and with a congregational polity, the church without a high doctrine of the Holy Spirit is not a pretty picture! In practice, what might this shift look like? What difference does it make to shift from democracy, and its assumptions, to discernment?

When I came to the congregation I currently serve, a fight was raging. The issue was the congregation's endowment fund and "divestment" from companies doing business in South Africa during the era of apartheid. The congregation had committed to and practiced "divestment," but not as scrupulously as some wished and advocated. The congregation's Annual Meeting had been picketed by some of its own members, a spectacle that had been carried on local television. Feelings ran high! Prior to my call, members of the Search Committee had described to me what they had experienced as the "loss of a sense of community" in the congregation during the years of this conflict. They also noted, in passing, that the congregation had five worship services at the time, not because of overcrowding (the one sanctuary service was normally about half full), but because different services appealed to different tastes and musical preferences. I discovered that only two of the services included a sermon.

My comment was this: "I would think it would be difficult to find your way in such a conflict without the shared experience of Word and Sacrament." Or to put it another way, preaching and the sacraments — at that moment in the life of that congregation — should speak, both explicitly and implicitly, to the burning issue in the church's life. Preaching at such a moment in a congregation's life need not harp on the issues week by week; but it needs to provide both a theological and pastoral perspective and grounding at critical points. Moreover, baptism is the reminder that we all enter the community of faith by the gift of grace, not ethical achievement. And the celebration of Holy Communion is, among other things, the invitation to "discern the Body" (I Corinthians 11:27). By "discern the Body," Paul meant that we should see and attend to others in the community of faith and to the needs of the whole membership of the church, which is the Body of Christ.

It is my observation that often, in the midst of congregational conflict, we forget the ways in which worship and sacrament would remind us of an identity and unity that transcend, and in some sense permit, our differences. Not unlike the early Corinthian congregation that Paul addressed in his letters, we divide into factions. Our own faction we regard as "the enlightened" or "more spiritual" or "more truly Christian." Those with whom we disagree, and are at odds with, are "the unenlightened," or "the sub-Christian." In such situations Paul calls upon the image of the church as "the Body of Christ." None of us, claims Paul, is the whole of the Body; we are parts of the Body. As parts we depend on one another and need one another, not despite our differences but precisely because of those differences. "Can you discern the Body?" asks Paul. Can you notice, acknowledge, and learn from others? Can we see that there is a whole that is larger than any one part?

Worship creates, at least potentially, the vessel that is capable of holding us in the midst of conflict. The point is not to say, in worship, "There, there, let's all just get along." It is to be reminded in the midst of conflict, which is both inevitable and sometimes life-giving, of a deeper unity and of a larger framework by which we are held together even as we struggle to discern the guiding of the Spirit regarding a particular issue. The grounds for the shift from democracy to discernment lie in life together as a worshiping community, and in building the bridge between our meetings for worship and our meetings for decision-making and business. In many ways, the shift from democracy to discernment may mean that our "business meetings" come to look and feel more like worship.

Another aspect of what Paul suggests in I Corinthians, and which contributes to the process and spirit of discernment, is that he teaches us that "the group (or congregation) has a life too." This is a phrase I learned in another context — while working on a multidisciplinary hospital oncology team. On this team, with people representing and speaking from many perspectives — oncology, nursing, social work, pastoral care, nutrition, and psychiatry — we were very much aware of our different perspectives. We were, to use Paul's language, aware of being "parts" of the body. One of our members took it as her task to remind us that we were not only parts, with the accountability and perspective of our particular disciplines; we also were, together, a group or a team. We had a responsibility to the group as well as to our individual perspectives. Hence, as this member of the team would occasionally observe, "The group has a life, too."

In the heat of congregational decision-making and disagreement we are apt to forget that "the group has a life too." We want to declare our views and score our points. Fine. But the group — the congregation — has a life, too. How are we supporting the life of the group? How are we diminishing it? This insight also contributes to the shift from democracy to discernment. The point is not just to express what we think, but to support the life of the congregation as we do so.

A further element in the move from democracy to discernment is to teach about the differences between decision-making and discernment. In the average congregation, many people have had considerable experience with decision-making. They understand debate, parliamentary procedure, motions, amendments, and voting. There are some, however, who do not understand all this or do not function well within such norms and procedures — sometimes because of differences in cultural background. Sometimes it is simply that they are less verbally adroit, or they prize verbal adroitness less than others do. Such people tend to become marginalized when Roberts Rules, rather than the Holy Spirit, rules. Some of those who have been relegated to the margins may become our teachers as we shift from democracy to discernment.

Sitting in at a recent meeting of a small congregation was a nine-year-old boy, Joshua. The congregation had been struggling for survival for some time and was debating whether or not to close its doors. The discussion went back and forth for some time. Some said that the wise thing to do was give the church a decent burial; others proposed new ways of going about the church's life and ministry. As a child, Joshua was not invited to speak, until there was a lull in the discussion, and no one knew what to say or do next. Someone in the group turned to Joshua and said, "What do you think, Joshua?" The boy thought for a moment and then said, "You're going to need the Bible. And you're going to have to be brave." It became clear that the Holy Spirit had chosen to speak to that church through a child.

In the average congregation there is considerable experience with democratic decision-making and parliamentary procedures. But members of those same congregations are less likely to understand discernment. Teaching about discernment as a spiritual practice will be important. Discernment involves listening to one another and listening for the Spirit. Moreover, as we listen to one another, the point is not necessarily to identify the will of the majority but to discern the mind of Christ and the will of God. "Attitude," goes the saying, "is everything." In this case, the attitude with which we approach our work and life together makes a great deal of difference. Do we seek the will of the majority or the mind of Christ?

So often we who have been steeped in the traditions of Western culture are eager to "get on with on it." "Let's study the facts, make a recommendation, and reach a decision," we say, reflecting the experience that guides us in much of life. There are certainly times and places for this attitude. But different norms and different sources inform the church. Discernment often takes time. Instead of rushing to decision and action, or assuming that we are ready to do so, we may need to step back, to engage in prayer, in Bible study, in worship, that we may better discern where the Spirit is leading. Thus, in the matter of the conflict cited above (over divestment in South Africa), we stepped back for a time, six months, to ground ourselves more nearly in worship, prayer, and the study of the Scripture. We emphasized the differences between spiritual discernment and other forms of decision-making.

Another example is drawn from the partnership of our congregation (predominantly European-American) with an African-American congregation, a partnership formed in the wake of the Rodney King incident in the early 1990s. Our congregation tended to employ democratic methods and procedures for decision-making. Moreover, we expected to come together with people from our partner congregation, pool our ideas, come up with a program and recommendations, and move toward implementation. We were frustrated and not a little confused that other norms, norms we did not seem to understand or even be able to quite grasp, seemed to be operating in the other congregation. When we were ready for action, they suggested that maybe we could study the Bible and pray together. When we expected a decision to be reached, they suggested that we might "wait on the Spirit a bit, wait to see what the Spirit might be saying to us." Such practices did not mean perpetual inaction; but it did mean a deepened awareness that we were not the only actors, and not the ones in charge.

It was a different but instructive approach. Some of us began to realize that the standard norms of decision-making that we observed might actually be a way of "quenching the Spirit," as Paul says. There wasn't a lot of room left for the Spirit to work when the agenda was printed, the time for discussion and debate was established, and the action items were all noted.

In working with a conflict in his congregation, a colleague describes the differences that such an approach — discernment — made. He notes that "numerous gatherings were held in which people were invited to listen to one another and to listen for the Spirit. We made room for silence and asked people to wait upon the Spirit through the silence. We not only began and ended gatherings in prayer, there were also times when we stopped for prayer in the midst of a gathering when someone felt led to offer one. During congregational meetings, we invited people to respond to each person's words by saying, 'May the Holy Spirit speak through us.' When people asked when we were going to take a vote, we told them that we didn't know and invited them to join us in waiting for further direction from the Spirit."

In both of these instances, people began to sense and experience the difference between decision-making as informed by democratic norms and the process of spiritual discernment. The experiences themselves proved to be formative — spiritually formative — which is not something that many say about the ordinary "business meetings" of the church. But they experienced something different: their process overcame the usual, false distinctions between the "spiritual life" and "business life" of the church. People on both sides of the question described the process of discernment as spiritually significant and formative for them.

In this new time, the church has the opportunity to rediscover and reclaim its own sources and wisdom, which are not identical with Western cultural norms and values. This is not to say that this tradition itself is without value; it certainly does have value. But secularized governance and decision-making processes miss a crucial opportunity for faith growth and spiritual formation. Earlier I observed that, in everything it is and everything it does, the church teaches. Engaging in such spiritual discernment within the life of the congregation seizes these experiences and processes as "teachable moments."

CHAPTER TEN

The Budget: From End to Means

During the era of Christendom, the mainline Protestant churches became accustomed to established status. Often that meant that maintaining the status quo was a sufficient goal and reason for our existence. There were, to be sure, eras of growth, vision, and expansion. The last was probably the effort to plant new churches in emerging suburbs in the 1950s and 60s, and the corollary effort during those baby-boom years to build or enlarge Christian Education wings, buildings, and facilities. But since the late 1960s, many mainline churches and denominations have been content to survive — or try to.

The corollary of this in terms of congregational budgets was that "meeting the budget," or "making the budget," became the annual rallying cry. Less often did we hear a call to more ambitious goals, such as "build a church," "start a new ministry," "build a hospital." This diminished sense of vision is among the surest signs that the church has ceased to be anything resembling a movement. It has become, instead, a settled institution. Nor does it require extended reflection to see that "making the budget" is a battle cry for institutional insiders. It is not one likely to capture the imagination of those not already committed to the institution. Another way to put this is that the budget often became an end rather than a means.

Often, as congregations became less goal- and mission-driven, the budget and budget processes became, ironically, more complex and arcane. Charts, pies, lists, lines, funds (some visible, some hidden), and associated turf battles came to characterize the annual slicing of the pie.

It was a classic case of "work avoidance." Rather than asking the important questions, we micromanaged the budget! When this becomes the case, chances are good that congregations have forgotten — or been afraid to ask — the prior questions. What is God calling us to be and to do? What is our purpose as a church? What are we trying to accomplish? What is our business?

If mainline congregations are to meet the adaptive challenge of the end of Christendom and the curtailment of our established status, we will need to learn again how to see the budget as a means rather than an end. The point is not to "make the budget"; the point is to ask, "What is our purpose as a church at this time and in this place, and what kinds of financial resources do we need to fulfill that purpose?" A budget is really a planning and administrative tool — and nothing more. In this new time, we are challenged to break the pattern of letting the budget take on a reified status and instead seek to allow God's Spirit to direct what is possible, and then seek the resources to accomplish it.

There is a deep spiritual issue here. When we allow the congregation's budget to become an end in itself, we have often succeeded in creating a system that acts as if God did not exist! What I mean by that is this: we do not ask the central questions nor practice discernment about what we are called to do. We simply maintain — with adjustments for cost-of-living and repairs. Really, you don't need God for that. But if, on the other hand, your first questions are about what God is calling you to do, and your second questions are about seeking the funding to do it, both questions can draw you deep into a process of faith formation.

The first question is one of discernment. As suggested above, this is an experience that is often difficult for people who are used to being self-reliant and in charge, which is of course the point. It is not about us. It is not about what we want to do, or don't want to do. It is about God and what God is trying to do in us and through us. To begin to ask those questions, to let God be God for us, is a challenging and risky adventure. Moreover, it is one that links the question of financial resources to the worship, preaching, teaching, and community life ministries of the church. What do we hear there? What do we discern as a worshiping people?

The second-level questions also become potentially formative of faith. If the first question is "What is God calling us to do?" the second is about seeking the funds that are needed. This gives us the opportunity to be in the role of both givers and receivers. It gives us the opportunity to learn to rely on God because, if we're lucky, we don't quite know where the resources will come from. I recall the night before a small congregation I was serving launched its first-ever capital funds drive. The church had been through some troubling times and had lost many members and much confidence. Still, the building — long neglected — was in serious and immediate need of repair. So we went through the steps leading up to a capital drive. But when the night before arrived, and the group that had given leadership and planned the work gathered, there was a great sense of foreboding. How could this little congregation of students and elderly people possibly meet this goal? What in the world were we thinking about when we committed ourselves to this path?

Clearly, we had been fools and were soon to be revealed as such in public! In truth, however, it was a great moment. We knew, even without quite being able to articulate it, that our own strength was not sufficient, that our own resources were not enough. We knew our need for God. So that night we prayed. Not the formal nods of prayer with which most meetings begin, but earnest, heartfelt, and somewhat desperate prayer. Aware — perhaps for the first time — of our own inadequacy, we gave God a chance to use us. We gave ourselves a chance to depend on God.

When we behave like established institutions and do not ask the key questions, and when we do not dare anything great for God, the entire budget exercise loses its promise and its possibility for being spiritually alive and formative. So a great deal is at stake in what some may dismiss as "only the budget" or "just the numbers." How are congregations to move from treating the budget as an end to understanding it as a means? It is not easy. Especially in long-established congregations, it is a tremendous challenge and one that must be worked at steadily over time. Still, it is not something we work at in a vacuum. It is, as I have suggested, related to worship, preaching, teaching, and other formative ministries in the life of a congregation. Perhaps a first step, then, is to punch holes in the artificial barriers that we often erect between "the spiritual life" and "the business life" of the church.

Another helpful step can be to use some form of strategic planning process that invites and allows for discernment. The guiding questions in such a process need to be the ones enumerated above. "What is God calling us to be and to do?" "What is our purpose?" "What are we trying to accomplish?" "What is our business?" In recent years, our congregation has found it helpful to do such planning work about every five years. In a variety of ways, the congregation is asked to participate in developing a five-year plan, or set of directions. It really is a congregational discernment process.

Such a process can help a congregation perceive what the current use of its resources indicates in the way of purpose and objectives. And it can allow redirection of resources in relation to new or more clearly focused purposes. But most of all, such a process and its outcome in a strategic plan helps a congregation move from "Okay, gang, let's make the budget!" to being able to articulate mission and ministry goals. Whether the mission and ministry goals are a strengthened music ministry, a new youth program for junior-high age, or maintaining an important ministry for frail elderly, the capacity to articulate what God calls us to is critical for a congregation's self-understanding as well as its capacity to appeal to more than institutional insiders.

Often when we seek to answer the question "What are you trying to accomplish?" we utilize some combination of ongoing ministries and new initiatives. There are some things that the church, if it is the church, will always be engaged in doing. In many ways these are described by the classic marks of the church: *kerygma* (worship and celebration), *didache* (teaching and learning), *koinonia* (community and care), and *diakonia* (service and witness). These provide a basic structure for beginning to describe a congregation's mission and ministry. These can be described as "the four core ministries of most congregations." And the overriding purpose of the four is Christian formation.

Beyond the four core ministries, congregations will perceive a call to timely new initiatives. Some, in time, will find their place in the four core ministries; others will exist for a period of time and then cease. The budget, however, becomes a means to accomplishing these four core ministries of the church and those new initiatives that reflect a particular and timely response to God's call and grace.

The Three-Legged Stool of Congregational Finance

A useful tool for thinking about a congregation's financial resources is the image of the three-legged stool. If the stool is to stand, all three legs need to be in place — and preferably the same height! The three legs of the stool are: (1) support for the annual operating budget; (2) an endowment; and (3) periodic capital drives.

Thus far in this chapter I have been focusing mainly on the first leg — support for the annual operating budget of the congregation. As we move from the established status of the Christendom era, it is critical that the budget become a means rather than an end. Most people will be supporting the annual operating budget from their current income. This creates an opportunity for a congregation to discuss annually a matter that is central to the spiritual life: money. What does money mean and symbolize for us? How do we use it? What is the relationship between our values and how we use money? Again, these are crucial *spiritual* issues and opportunities. I thank God that the church has helped me learn the practice of regular and significant giving. It is the only way that wealthy people — and by global standards all North Americans are very wealthy — will gain some degree of freedom in this area of our lives. Only by giving money away will we have enough. It is a gospel paradox.

The second leg of the stool, endowments, is a problematic one in the eyes of many Christians who believe that the church should not have accumulated resources or funds. There is much to be said for this argument. Endowments are, without a doubt, a great challenge, both a blessing and a curse. But there are also good reasons for this leg of the stool. One is that many people in North America do have accumulated assets, often more than anticipated. A planned giving program can help members of a congregation come to grips with those assets and their use. How is my "estate" to be used when I die? Can the values and commitments that have been important to me in my lifetime somehow be reflected in the way these assets are used after I am gone? These are important questions to ask — and for people to struggle with. One reason for an endowment, which will be funded not from people's annual incomes but from accumulated assets, is to raise these questions.

Another, and perhaps the central reason, for a planned giving program or endowment as one leg of the stool of congregational financial resources is that it does challenge a congregation to stretch its vision and expand its mission. It raises the questions that we have asked regarding the budget. Or, put positively, it allows the congregation to enlarge its mission. Beneath some expressed fears about an endowment is something like the fearful timidity of the servant who received one talent in the parable (Matthew 25:14-30). So fearful was that servant that he buried the talent rather than use it. Sometimes congregations and their leaders are most comfortable with a hand-to-mouth existence (even though individuals and families in the congregation are well off), because then nothing much is expected. "To whom much is given, of him much will be expected" (Luke 12:48).

In some ways, congregations that have an endowment may be in the best position to talk honestly with rich North Americans about the responsibilities and opportunities that come with such resources. Make no mistake, it is a challenge to use such resources well and faithfully, but the fact that it is a challenge does not mean it should be avoided. It is a challenge that many families and individuals in our congregations are facing. When a church faces this challenge honestly and well, it can be a tremendous teaching opportunity for the congregation and its members!

Endowments are often thought to be the creation of the very wealthy. In our congregation we discovered that an endowment that had grown to twenty million dollars was the result of gifts and bequests that averaged $11,000! It was the creation, not of the fabulously wealthy, but of widows, schoolteachers, small-business people, musicians, social workers, and attorneys, among others, who loved their church and deepened their own sense of meaning in life by making such a bequest. As such, an endowment is a very tangible reminder of what the epistle to the Hebrews speaks of as "the great cloud of witnesses." Our congregation tries to make the sense of that "great cloud of witnesses" real by an annual gathering to remember and tell the stories of those departed ones who supported the endowment, and to thank all those who have made their own plan to do so. We recall the stories of Grace, Ruth, Harold, Peggy, Win, and a hundred others to remind ourselves that the endowment is the creation of actual people, people like us.

The third leg of the stool is periodic capital fund drives. By definition, capital fund drives are concerned with the bricks and mortar, the "fixed assets," and not the ongoing funding of particular programs. I have known congregations and ministers who take pride in never having such fund drives — thus allowing the buildings their congregations occupy to decline and become eyesores. "We don't have an edifice complex! We put it all into mission!" is the refrain of these congregations and their leaders — with no small hint of pride. What they fail to see is that the whole life of the church, in this new era, is mission. To be sure, church structures can be overbuilt. But more often today, mainline congregations are either underbuilt or poorly maintained. The message such facilities convey is not, generally, a great commitment to mission or outreach but a lack of care and appropriate self-confidence.

Periodic capital drives (how often "periodic" is depends on local needs and situations, but every ten years is probably about right), also provide newcomers and new generations a chance for "buy-in" and investment of themselves. If all the building work has been done by previous generations, new generations will tend to have less investment and ownership in the life of the church than might otherwise be the case. Clearly, capital drives must be undertaken for legitimate needs and goals; but when those are clear, they do create an opportunity for a congregation to ask the crucial questions of mission and purpose and how their plant and facilities do or do not serve those purposes.

Today many mainline congregations have pulled in their sails and drawn into port. Too many are content, at best, to maintain the vessel without daring any new voyage. The old saw remains true: "Nothing ventured, nothing gained." Developing financial resources with a strong three-legged stool is never something done for its own sake. It is done for the sake of the thing God is calling us to do and to be in our time. The challenge is to risk asking those questions afresh and then setting out in response to God's new call to mission and ministry. The budget is not the issue, nor is it the end; it is but a tool and a means. The end questions, those about purpose, are the ones that need to be engaged courageously if we are to respond to the adaptive challenge posed by the end of the Christendom era.

CHAPTER ELEVEN

From Fellowship to Hospitality

"The true and real sacrament of the Protestant church," observed one wag, "is the coffee hour." When church is out, coffee is on and people gather in fellowship halls across the land for what we have come to designate as "fellowship." Of course, "fellowship" in its origins is not as pallid or superficial as the typical church coffee hour may seem to be. The Greek word *koinonia* bespeaks a kind of bond, an affection, a unity that is deep and enduring, not superficial and episodic.

Not only has fellowship been thinned out to the coffee-hour experience, but congregations have come to judge and rate themselves on their "friendliness": "We are," say many congregations, "a friendly church." To not be "friendly" is to be a bad thing, a failure as a church. But are friendliness and fellowship all that they are held up to be? Too often, I suspect, what we mean by fellowship and a friendly church is that we find people like ourselves in that church. We find the church full of people of our social group, educational background, lifestyle, values, and so on. When we find compatible people, we deem the church to be friendly, comfortable, and "a good fit."

The danger in all this emphasis on fellowship and friendliness of similar and like-minded people is that the church is fast on its way to becoming a club or a clan rather than a church. The danger is that we mistake our earthen vessels (II Corinthians 4) of race, culture, and lifestyle for the transcendent power of God. The danger is that in our close-knit fellowship, our friendly church, there is no room for God, who comes to us as the stranger, the outsider. The danger is that our friendly churches have no room for the God who is, often as not, intrusive, disruptive, and not always "friendly"! Instead of aiming to be a friendly church, perhaps we ought to hope to be a church that practices hospitality. In the world and times of American Christendom, where North American society was more homogeneous and less pluralistic, friendliness may have made a certain amount of sense. But this new time calls for a rediscovery and reclaiming of hospitality.

Hospitality is a very different concept than friendliness. According to John McFadden, "When we extend hospitality to the stranger, we make no assumption that this person will have anything at all in common with us, much less that we will like one another. It could be someone unpleasant, even dangerous; we are still obligated to offer our hospitality." In these ways hospitality is at odds with friendliness. Typically, being friendly grows out of the idea that the person we are meeting will have a lot in common with us. If we just take the trouble to get to know him or her, we will soon be friends. As an old saying goes, "There are no strangers, only friends we haven't met yet." If we get to know one another, I will discover that I like you and you will like me. Moreover, we will find that we have a lot in common, that we are really very much the same.

But what happens when that does not work? What happens when the guest or stranger is of another faith or race and refuses to relinquish his or her particularity in the interest of "getting along" and "fitting in"? What happens when the guest or stranger is someone who has been living on the streets for a week or a year and looks and smells awful? What happens when the guest or the stranger is a convicted criminal or a sex offender?

Hospitality does not rest on the assumption that we are all the same, or that in getting to know someone we will find that we will really like that person. Hospitality allows the other to be other, to be different. The biblical origins and stories of hospitality are many. Sarah and Abraham welcomed passing strangers, inviting them to rest and eat with them. It turned out that one of the strangers was God himself, who had come to announce to the old folks that they would have a child, their first, before the year was out. Even that was not a particularly welcome, or easy, message. Later in the Genesis story, the judgment of God comes down on Sodom and Gomorrah — not, as some have argued, because of sex, but because of a failure of hospitality. The citizens of those famous cities abused the guests and strangers in their midst.

The New Testament begins, one might say, with a story of hospitality — or failed hospitality. When Joseph and Mary journey to Bethlehem to be counted in the Roman census, they find that there is "no room for them" at the inn. They take shelter in a cattle shed, or cave. The innkeeper has unwittingly turned away the Son of God, an act that foreshadows the way the world will prove inhospitable to a God whose ways are strange to us.

The practice of hospitality is at the heart of the biblical faith, but not simply because it is a good thing to do. It is at the heart of the biblical faith because, as the letter to the Hebrews puts it, "In welcoming the stranger, you may entertain angels unawares." What is at stake in hospitality is welcoming God. And what can be lost when the church becomes a club, a "friendly church" with lots of fellowship, is the presence of God coming at us through the stranger, the guest, the unexpected one.

"In some churches," writes John McFadden, "there is an emphasis — even an insistence — that all members believe the same way, live the same way, vote the same way. A friend of mine calls these 'cookie cutter Christian' churches because they tend to stamp out members who are carbon copies of one another. After awhile, the members of such churches even begin to look like each other!

"These churches have a way of justifying their uniformity. They quote scripture to demonstrate that 'all brethren should be of one mind' or insist that there can only be one correct doctrine and one proper way for Christians to live. They seem to think it is their mission to force all members to conform to a single identity."

A different way might be described as a church with a clear center but open boundaries. Rather than drawing a hard line that says who is in and who is out, the centered church articulates and honors its center in the Lordship of Jesus Christ. But the walls have many doors. The boundaries are porous. Whoever is moving toward the center is welcome, no matter how far from the center they may be coming from. In such a church the goal is not to foster uniformity. It is to receive those whom God sends us. It is to foster in all people their own unique expression of Christ and their own specific God-given gifts for ministry. "The more diversity we can welcome into the community of the church," observes a colleague, "the more of Christ we can reveal — to one another and to the world."

If our unity does not lie in the church, in our sociological, political, economic, or philosophical similarities to one another, then where does it lie? Where is it to be found? It is to be found in God, and in God's gift of baptism, by which "all are made one in Christ." Jew and Greek (ethnic and racial differences), male and female (gender differences), rich and poor (economic differences) — all cease to matter, Paul tells the Galatians. This points the way to the practice of hospitality. Differences are real; we are not all the same. But differences can be, and have been by God's act in Christ, transcended. Barriers have been broken down. Hostility has been overcome.

If part of the shift for congregations in the new postmodern era is from fellowship and friendliness to hospitality, what might that look like in practice? What specific ways are people in congregations helped to practice hospitality?

The congregation I serve is located in an urban downtown. One of our commitments is that the church building be open, not locked, during the day. It is accessible to all who wish to enter. One does not have to be buzzed in or need to punch in a key code to enter. This has, of course, resulted in problems: occasionally thefts and vandalism occur. One year a porcelain manger scene was even stolen from the church! And it might be that, with particular kinds of threats or problems, we would have to reexamine this policy or change it. But in some ways the literal and physical openness of the church building is also symbolic — symbolic to the world around us and to the congregation itself. We have tried to communicate to ourselves and to others a combination of commitments that is expressed by our open doors: namely, we seek to be a church that is centered, that has a clear center in Christ, and a church that is open and hospitable. These commitments are not at odds with the gospel; rather, they are another of the gospel's paradoxes. A clear center in Christ allows openness and receptivity, and our open doors express this commitment.

Another way in which a commitment to hospitality becomes real for us is in what we have come to call our Companion's Ministry. Again, because we are a downtown congregation, we frequently have in our midst those who are homeless and those who are suffering from chronic or acute mental illness. We have sought to respond to these particular needs in long-term ways. The congregation has a low-income housing ministry with nine buildings and 600-some units of housing; it also has a mental health ministry. But these are long-term responses. On Sunday mornings we have one or two "companions" on duty. The companions have received training for their ministry of being a presence with people who have special needs, or acute anxiety, or are experiencing distress. When these symptoms are signaled by words or behavior, the companion on duty reaches out to those in need, offering to sit with them, to share a cup of coffee, to listen, and, when appropriate, to guide them to help. This allows our congregation to welcome the stranger who may be in distress.

Part of our hospitality is that there are limits and boundaries. If a person is violent, we will call the police. If a person is drunk or belligerent, he or she may be asked to leave until he or she is ready to come back another time. If a person is disruptive, we point out that others are present and their needs too deserve acknowledgment and respect.

To support the Companions Ministry there are periodic training events and classes in the ministry of presence. These help people to gain skills in listening, in diffusing conflict, in asking questions that are not invasive, in becoming aware of existing facilities and programs for help, and in how to respond to emergencies.

Another way in which we encourage hospitality is in periodically helping the congregation to look at the church through the eyes of a guest or a stranger. The person who is there for the first time sees things (and does not see things) that others, who are in the church building and congregation on a regular basis, do not see. What obstacles are there to finding your way around? Is it clear and evident where parking and bathrooms are to be found? How do people know what to do to participate in the worship service?

We have found it helpful to do an occasional skit that helps people see the church and congregation through the eyes of the stranger or guest. Sometimes a relative newcomer will write an article for the newsletter noting how they have experienced hospitality or not. There are periodic reminders that when we gather on Sunday mornings we are called to welcome the stranger among us. We are called to welcome those God has sent to us, not because we want them to "join the club," but because in some way God would seek to become present to us through that person.

Another step toward hospitality is what we call our "Faith Journey" series. Every summer Sunday a member of the congregation is invited to share the story of his or her faith. What has shaped that faith? What has challenged it? What people and experiences have been especially important to you in the formation and growth of your faith? How have you experienced God's presence, and absence, in your life? What are your faith affirmations at this point on the journey? And what are your questions?

In each "Faith Journey" the speaker usually talks for thirty to forty minutes, followed by ten to twenty minutes for response from those in attendance. This series contributes to a sense and ministry of hospitality in the congregation in several ways. First of all, it creates a space in which the person who is relating his or her story has the chance to do so. Hospitality is often about creating a space, a safe space, in which another can share their gifts. Second, the sharing which people do is generally honest and includes a fair amount of self-disclosure. This has a way of saying to those who are present that I too can be honest here. Third, the Faith Journey series gives the guest or stranger among us the chance to hear in an in-depth way about matters of faith from members of the congregation, and not just the clergy. In this way, it is a real insight into the life of the congregation and those who make it up.

Still another way in which hospitality is practiced in this particular congregation is in relation to partnerships with other congregations. I have previously mentioned such a relationship with a predominantly African-American congregation. Through that relationship members of the two congregations have met for Bible study and prayer, have worked together in ministries of service, and welcomed one another's pastors and choirs in their own services of worship.

Our congregation also has a long-standing and vibrant partnership with a congregation in Managua, Nicaragua. Groups from our congregation visit in Nicaragua, and we welcome guests from that congregation. A particular form of hospitality that has been fostered by the partnership has been an ongoing Spanish language group or class in our congregation. We have also learned to sing hymns in Spanish. In an increasingly multicultural world such efforts to learn the language of another country and culture are an important sign and act of hospitality.

In the Gospel of Luke, Jesus comes to two of his disciples as a stranger. He walks alongside them as they trudge back to their home in the small town of Emmaus after the crucifixion. Even when he speaks to them and begins to explain the Scriptures they do not recognize that it is Jesus. But later they invite him to be their guest, to join them in their home for food and shelter because night is coming on. So Jesus joins them as their guest. But then a strange thing happens. The guest becomes the host as Jesus takes the bread that is on the table, breaks it, and shares it with them. In their act of hospitality, they have allowed Jesus to share his gifts with them, even to become their host. Hospitality allows another to share the gifts which they bear, and at least sometimes the gift they bear to us is the very presence of God!

CHAPTER TWELVE

Membership Growth: From Passive to Active

I've saved this one for last, not because it is the best but because it is the one that is so often the very first in the concerns of congregations and church leaders. "We're aging, we're shrinking," cry mainline congregations. "How can we grow?" "Can we grow?" "What's wrong with us that we aren't growing?" These are often the somewhat desperate kinds of questions and anxieties that fuel attempts at change or renewal in the mainline churches. They are valid questions and concerns, but they should not be our first concern.

Membership growth is, in many ways, a by-product of effective ministry and mission, and not its goal. Thus I discuss this last among the shifts in congregational culture that I have considered and described. I am convinced that growth in membership will happen for congregations that are engaged in the other shifts and changes I have described in preceding chapters. That is, membership growth will come out of other kinds of growth. Or to put it negatively, if these other kinds of growth are not happening, membership growth will either be very short-lived or will not take place at all. To this initial caveat about membership growth — that it is not the goal, but a result of vital congregations — I would add several other caveats about membership growth.

First, as Loren Mead and others have pointed out, growth takes a variety of forms. Growth in attendance or in numbers of members is not the only form of growth a congregation can experience. Congregations can grow, as well, in faith. Their understanding of the faith, their experience of the sacred, and their practice of Christianity can be deepened. Congregations can also grow in mission and service. They rise to some new occasion, take a risk to establish and support a new venture of caring for the neighbor in need.

A second and related caveat about membership growth: it does have something to do with the setting and demographics of a congregation. It is no accident that most of the mega-churches are based in the newer, rapidly growing suburbs; they have located where the greatest population growth is occurring. A century ago, and in the post–World War II era, mainline congregations did the same. Only now the city and town centers and the older suburbs, where most mainline congregations are located, are no longer where the population growth is taking place. It is often just the opposite. Population is stable, or it is declining — and it is aging. This is a genuine factor in membership growth; but while it must be taken into account, it does not constitute a reason or excuse for accepting no growth or a decline in membership. We have to be realistic about location, but it is not the only factor at work.

A third caveat about membership growth is similar to my first point: that membership growth is a result and not the goal of a congregation's life and vitality. I agree with Kirk Hadaway that our goal in congregations is not necessarily to be large churches or even to be great churches, but rather to be real churches. By "real" Hadaway means communities of faith where the sacred is experienced in life-transforming ways, and where the Christian faith becomes incarnate in the life of a congregation and its members. Many congregations seem to have the idea that when they get big, when they "grow up," then they will be real churches. That is mistaken. We have it on reliable authority that a real church can be composed of as few as two or three. Again, growth is not the goal but a possible by-product or result of being a real church.

With all these caveats and qualifiers out on the table, it must be said that membership growth does have a place and significance. Especially in a time when too many congregations have become clubs or clans that are dedicated to the contentment of their members, growth in membership is one indication that a congregation is not simply a club. Clubs tend to take in enough new members to meet their own needs, to pay the bills, to fill out the committees, and to add "people like us." Churches, on the other hand, grow because they are engaged in the movement of human transformation, of healing, of new life and

change. While all the caveats about growth — the varieties of
"growth," the importance of congregational setting and demographics,
and growth as a by-product and result, not a goal — remain true, one
of the reasons that many, if not most, mainline congregations have
been either stable or declining in the last forty years is that they have
been better clubs than churches. Membership growth, or growth in attendance and participation in the congregation's life, is certainly one
sign of vitality and faithfulness. Growth happens where lives are being
changed, and in all likelihood that growth will involve the vitality of
engagement in ministry.

Moreover, membership growth also fits the pattern underlying all
the shifts in congregational culture that I have discussed. In all ten
shifts we can see how the church in the Christendom and modern eras
took a certain shape. In all ten it is also possible to see how a different
shape and focus is required in this new time. From the standpoint of
membership growth, the mainline Protestant churches tended, in the
Christendom era, to have what might be called a "guaranteed market
share." Sure, we had to integrate and assimilate new members, but as
the religious establishment we didn't have to worry too much about
where they would come from. We were a bit like the town bank. Remember the town bank? In the community where I served my first
church, a small town in the foothills of the Cascade Mountains in western Washington, there was one bank in town, which, like the church,
stood on Main Street. The town bank pretty much had a lock on business, on the market in that small town. In a certain sense, the church
also had a lock on business, on the market in that small town.

In the intervening years, two successive mergers have swallowed up
that town bank. It has lost its local pedigree and identification. Moreover, there are other banking options: new banks have opened in nearby
towns and growing suburbs; ATM machines of other banks are now
available in town; some people do their banking online. No longer is it
"the town bank" in the same sense that was true for decades. It is one
option among many. In somewhat the same sense, the mainline
Protestant churches have become one option among many. There are
other churches in town and in the nearby, growing suburbs; there are
other forms and styles of spirituality; and there are the ATMs, so to
speak, of the self-help spiritual gurus and the online forms of religion
on television, cable, and Internet.

When mainline Protestant congregations were the religious establishment of North American culture and the center of community and family life, we didn't worry much about membership growth or market share. Our approach to membership growth was a passive one, like that of the town bank. But today banks that don't concern themselves with market share cease to exist. They can no longer assume that they will have business by virtue of history and location alone. The world of banks and financial institutions is a rapidly changing one. Banks no longer take a passive approach to customer service.

Like the town bank, mainline congregations can no longer assume that they have a constituency or base of participants simply by virtue of history and location. What matters is not being in the town the longest, or being on the right street corner, but delivering the goods. Being a vital congregation and a real church is what matters. Moreover, the new era requires a shift from a passive approach to membership growth — or growth in participation — to a more active one. The congregation I serve is, according to denominational studies, among those "most likely to be in decline" in terms of membership. The three factors identified as markers of a declining church are that they were established prior to 1900, that they are located in a city, and that the membership is more than half female. In those terms, our congregation has "three strikes" against it. We were founded in 1869, the second oldest congregation in Seattle; we are smack-dab in downtown; and we are about 60 percent female. And yet we are growing in membership — not wildly, not rapidly, but nonetheless growing. In the ten years between 1990 and 2000, we have grown more than 20 percent in worship attendance and 15 percent in membership. Among mainline Protestant congregations located in urban downtown locations, this is rapid growth!

What explains this? There is no one factor. The multiple shifts in congregational culture, described in previous chapters, have something to do with it. But, in addition to these factors, we have tried to cultivate a less passive, a more active, approach to membership and participation growth. The key concepts here are "invitation" and "sharing."

When asked to think about membership growth, many mainline Protestant church members assume that what is being asked of them is to get people to come to church and join up. Maybe that's too much to ask. And, just possibly, that assumes that it is all up to us. Whether people come and get changed and join up is not entirely in our hands.

It is up to them; and it is up to God. What is in our hands is the capacity to share something about our own experience and extend an invitation.

Sharing Our Experience of God

We have tried to help people find their own voices and words for sharing something of their experience of God in their lives. The primary emphasis is not on the church, but on God. How have they experienced the sacred in life-changing ways? Such sharing seems to work best in a conversational and dialogical style, rather than monologue. As we speak with others, we try to listen to their stories and share our own. Generally speaking, such sharing is not easy for mainline Protestants. It is not easy for us, but neither is it impossible.

Hearing their pastors speak of their own faith and of their experience of God is crucial to helping members of a congregation do this sharing. If clergy are not able or willing to speak in such ways about their own faith and experience, we can simply forget about it when it comes to most laity. But when clergy are able and willing to speak of their own faith and their experience of God in ways that are genuine, people listen and are given permission and examples for doing the same themselves.

Our congregation has also given laypeople explicit opportunities to try sharing their faith and experience of God. Each summer, ten or so people are asked to share their "faith journey" during the hour between services. They talk about their experiences of God's presence and God's absence. They talk about how their faith has changed, and how it has changed them. They talk about their convictions and their questions, their affirmations and their doubts. In addition to this annual "faith journey" series, we give parishioners a chance to practice by doing a similar, but more condensed, version in worship services. For example, during the season between Epiphany and Ash Wednesday, one person each week may be asked to talk for three to five minutes in response to the question, "Where have you experienced the presence of God in the ministries of this church?" Or, during Lent, people may talk about an experience of God's power or Christ's presence in the midst of loss or brokenness. The point is not perfection in sharing, not that anyone knows what perfection would look like. The point is permission — permission and practice.

Invitation, or "Come and See"

The second thing we have tried to do in our congregation is to say that we can share an invitation. It is not up to us to make people come or to compel them to join the church or to become Christians. It is ours to share an invitation. In the Gospel of John we find some simple, but helpful, words with which to share an invitation, the repeated invitation to discipleship in three words: "Come and see." As with most of the Fourth Gospel, the words have layers of meaning. At one level, they are simple and straightforward: come along and take a look. At another level, they are much more profound: come and have your eyes opened to a whole new world. Come and see what is really real. Just as the Fourth Gospel states the invitation while letting the levels of meaning stand without explanation, so too can we share such words with others.

To say "come and see" to a friend, colleague, or acquaintance does not require us to do a great deal. This is probably just as well. Most people don't need or even want a full statement of Christian convictions. A simple and genuine invitation will do. "Come, sometime, and see." How someone responds to that is up to him or her, and up to God. It is not up to us to make it happen; it is simply up to us to share an invitation. But here's the catch: "come and see" takes us back to the first and following shifts in congregational culture. In other words, if people take us up on the invitation and do come, what do they see and experience? Do they see a congregation doing a halfhearted civic faith? Or do they see a congregation engaged in the work of change and healing — of human transformation? If they come, do they see a congregation that "assumes the goods," i.e., where everyone sort of already knows God and knows what being a Christian means? Or do they see a congregation that is "delivering the goods"? A congregation where worship is alive and where people are engaged in faith development and ministry?

The Congregation as Evangelist

Another way to put this is to say that the primary agent of evangelism is the congregation itself. By "evangelism" I mean sharing the good news of the gospel, the good news about God and what God has done and is doing in Christ. For some, the evangelist is a particular person, a preacher; for others, the evangelist is a specific kind of ministry, one of bringing new people to faith. Both of these models have their place and legitimacy. But here is another option or model: the congregation itself is the evangelist. It is the congregation that embodies the good news. It is the congregation that forms people in this new life. It is the congregation that sustains people on the journey of Christian life, and it is the congregation that is the instrument through which God works transformation.

Thus we conclude this series of shifts in congregational culture where we began. What is the purpose of the church? The purpose, the business, of the church is to change people, to transform them. The congregation is the evangelist, the bearer of good news. When we say "come and see," we are saying something simple and straightforward. Come and take a look. We are also, like the Gospel of John, saying something that has deeper levels of meaning: "Come and get your eyes opened." "Come and see yourself — and others — and the world in a new way." "Come and follow Jesus." Ultimately, this is what it is about. Membership growth is a symptom, an important but secondary effect, of a congregation that participates in some measure in the new life of the kingdom of God.

When I have presented these shifts in congregational culture at conferences, classes, and workshops, the question people often ask is, "Okay, how do we get started?" "Where do we begin?" My answer is, "Begin where you are." That is, what I have said is not "ten steps to a new congregation"; this is simply what I have learned. What *you* learn and what *you* need to do may be different. It is not my intention to offer a package you can buy with this book and then put down in your congregation or setting. Would that it were that simple! It is not. This is not a how-to book. It is more like a report on what I have learned in responding to the great shift and the new age we face in the mainline Protestant churches.

And yet, there are some things to be said about next steps — about where we go from here. The concluding chapter focuses on leadership in the midst of adaptive change and challenge. What are some skills and strategies that help leaders guide congregations as they go about changing congregational culture?

CHAPTER THIRTEEN

Leadership for Change: Skills and Strategies

Observation and experience has led me to the conclusion that no single factor is more important to congregational vitality than leadership. Leadership matters. Yet, while leadership matters and is critical to congregational vitality, there is no one model or style of leadership that is normative or that fits all sizes and situations. How that leadership is shaped and exercised is open to multiple variations that fit the people, the congregation, and the context.

It is also true that leaders will do a variety of different tasks and fill a number of different roles. Not all leaders are equally able in every role or task, nor do they have to be. What leaders do need to be able to do, according to Rabbi Edwin Friedman, is to define themselves and their goals. Friedman calls this "self-differentiation": it is the capacity for self-definition, the ability of a leader "to define his or her own goals or values while trying to maintain a non-anxious presence within the system" that is critical. Leaders need to know who they are and what their convictions are. And they require the ability to be clear about their goals without becoming so anxious that they seek to force their goals on others or on a congregation.

Leaders not only need this capacity for self-definition; they also need to be able to, in Ron Heifetz's terms, "mobilize people for adaptive work." This means helping people recognize the adaptive challenges before them, as well as keeping the group or body focused on that adaptive work. Recently someone interviewed members of our congregation in order to understand their experience as members of the congregation and to identify the sources of the congregation's strength and vitality. All of those interviewed, independent of one another, indicated that "leadership" — of both clergy and laity — was the key factor in the congregation's vitality. Of my leadership, one of those interviewed commented, "He keeps the vision in our face all the time." That sounds a bit more aggressive than I might want to describe it myself; but it is an effective way of talking about keeping people focused on the central adaptive challenges. This is what leaders do. They help the people name and identify the challenges they face; and they help to mobilize the gifts, strength, courage, and resources necessary to respond to them. They keep attention focused on the task at hand.

Yet, despite the critical nature of leadership, many mainline clergy and congregations are ambivalent about leadership and are poorly led. For some years we mainline Protestants have been hearing about "facilitation," "empowerment," "shared ministry," and "team ministry." There is nothing wrong with any of these concepts. Effective leaders do these things: they work in teams; they share leadership; they empower others. Effective leadership facilitates the fulfillment of congregational goals and aspirations. But too often such concepts have been a verbal fog seemingly designed to mask our lack of clarity about the nature of effective leadership and the importance of leadership for the church.

Evidence of the lack of clarity and of our ambivalence is everywhere in the church today. Clergy have tried to shift leadership and responsibility to laity; laity, for their part, have tried to give it back to clergy. Clergy have doubted whether leadership was a part of their job. Congregations have resisted and undermined ministers who would exercise leadership. Often those entering the ministry receive little training in seminary — or anywhere else — in the area of leadership. It is not clear from seminary preparation that congregational leadership is a central task of the ordained minister. Often one encounters clergy and congregations who seem to view ordained ministers as chaplains to a congregation rather than leaders of a church. Moreover, and adding to the lack of clarity, there is a widespread fuzziness about the respective ministries of the ordained and lay. What does ordination mean? What are the ordained clergy ordained to? What is the ministry of the laity? What is the meaning of their baptism?

My conviction is that leadership is critical if congregations are to respond to the huge adaptive challenge faced by mainline churches. The leadership will, of necessity, be shared: both clergy and laity need to exercise leadership within congregations. But the primary responsibility as congregational leaders rests with the clergy; it is their calling to lead the church. The classic Reformed understanding of the ministries of the laity and the ordained provides help here. The ministry of the ordained, the Reformers held, is to equip the saints — the church — for ministry. This is done through preaching, teaching, sacramental ministry, and pastoral care. The ministry of the laity is to represent Christ to the world through their vocations and lives. Like coaches, the ordained lead, teach, and prepare the team for its games. The laity are the team that takes the field.

These are broad distinctions, not airtight compartments, and the distinctions cannot be pushed too far. But they do provide useful guidance. And making these distinctions helps us perceive that too often today they get completely turned around. Clergy try to take over the proper role of the laity in representing Christ to the world. They run around the community doing a little bit of everything and pronouncing on all manner of issues. Laity, for their part, try to take over the role of clergy in directing the life and ministries of the church — precisely the work the clergy have (at least in theory) been prepared to do. Thus we have the coach on the field, with a few of the team members on the sidelines, and most of the team sitting in the stands!

Give the ministry of representing Christ to the world back to the people. Get the team on the field of play. Give the ministry of leading the church back to ordained ministers, and get the coach working with the team. Both ministries are critical, and mutually dependent on one another, if the church is to be vital and faithful.

Six Strategies for Leaders

Given these convictions and parameters, how are congregational leaders to offer leadership in this new time? In his work, Ron Heifetz suggests a number of strategies for leadership in situations of adaptive challenge. I will draw on Heifetz's strategies as main categories and then enlarge on them with further examples and leadership skills from my own work and writing.

Strategy Number One: Getting to the Balcony

By "getting to the balcony," Heifetz has in mind the metaphor of a dance floor. On the floor, in the midst of the constant movement and swirl and sound, it is difficult to see what is going on, to detect the patterns of activity and relationship. For that, leaders need to get to the balcony. From up above, out of the fray, they have a chance to see the whole and detect patterns in it. Or to change the metaphor slightly, one needs to get off the playing field periodically and up above the sideline level, in order to see what is happening on the field. When you're in the midst of it, it's difficult to get the big picture.

For clergy and church leaders, getting up to the balcony may mean getting away from the congregation periodically — not just to forget about it but to see it more clearly. Sometimes a quiet retreat is useful; at other times a continuing education event can play this role. Visits to other congregations are also helpful, because they tend to bring differences and similarities into higher relief. It may not always be necessary to get away physically, sometimes merely to step back mentally.

When a leader gets to the balcony, what is she or he looking for? Patterns. Connections. Disconnections. From the balcony we look for patterns of relationships and interaction. Who engages whom? Who does not engage whom? What group affiliations shape patterns of interaction? Leaders are also looking for the patterns of group behavior. What are the patterns of interaction with the wider community? How does a congregation respond to conflict, or to new ideas? Where is leadership located? Who has power and influence? What are the sources of authority? How does a congregation interpret and understand itself? How does it tell its own story?

Another way to put all of this is to say that from the balcony leaders try to see the whole beyond the parts. They try, in the apostle Paul's phrase, to "discern the body," the Body of Christ, and to see not just the individuals but the group and the wholeness of its life. Some leaders and some clergy seem to have the capacity for getting the larger picture almost instinctively. Others have to work at it. Most will benefit from consulting with others who have a particular sensibility to such patterns and interactions. Some of those consultants will be found within the congregation; others may be invited in from the outside. Sometimes denominational officers or clergy colleagues who serve other churches are helpful. Sometimes consultants or trainers can stand with us in the balcony and point out what is going on.

Most of all, what leaders look for from the balcony are the gaps: the gaps between what a congregation claims as its core values and what is actually going on. Leaders also look for the norms and strategies that a congregation is accustomed to but that are no longer, in our new time, relevant or productive. These gaps help us identify the adaptive challenges we face.

Strategy Number Two: Identify the Adaptive Challenge

From the balcony, leaders begin to discern the patterns, the interactions, and the gaps that enable them to identify the adaptive challenges faced by a congregation. In the earlier chapters of this book I have suggested some ways of describing the broad adaptive challenge faced by mainline Protestant congregations no longer living in American Christendom. We are no longer citizens of the modern era, with its consensus story and its guiding values of self-sufficiency, reason, progress, and optimism. We live in a culture and society that is officially secular and religiously pluralistic. We are no longer the religious establishment, but one voice and perspective among many.

Beyond this, and in the chapters that trace "shifts in congregational culture," I have sought to name more specific adaptive challenges that follow from these broad changes in culture and society. Some of these will, I hope, help to illuminate and describe your particular situation and challenges. But this work is context-dependent. Each situation will offer different adaptive challenges or particular ways of framing those I have described. Moreover, this work is continuous: it does not get completed or finished, but goes on constantly. Thus, I will suggest here some skills for identifying adaptive challenges in your situation, and provide some further specific examples.

As congregational leaders seek to identify the adaptive challenges facing their own congregations, one important skill is that of asking questions. The question of purpose is central: it precedes in sequence and importance the matter of vision. Often, when anxiety is running high in the life of a congregation, people will ask for the vision. "Where are we going?" This may be a trap for the unwary leader. She or he seeks to answer the vision question, the "where are we going?" cry, and then people dig in their heels and say, "No way, we are not going there! You have the wrong vision, the wrong destination for us!" Prior to the vision question is the purpose question. What is the purpose of the church? Why are we here? What is a church for? What business are we in? How does what we say about our purpose get embodied in our life and ministry?

Asking the purpose question first helps leaders to avoid the trap of having to come up with the compelling vision. It is a way of giving the work back to the people. There is a time and place for shaping and communicating a compelling vision, but vision is derived from purpose. If we are not clear about why we are here, the vision becomes only another to-do list. I have found that another useful question for leaders who are seeking to identify the adaptive challenges is the "vital few" question. What are the vital few things that we as a church must do and do well if we are to accomplish our purpose? Many long-established congregations are spread too thin. Having lost clarity about purpose, they try to do everything that anybody thinks is a good idea. This results in the Pecos River phenomenon: it's a mile wide but only a foot deep! What are the vital few?

Another skill for identifying the adaptive challenges is to draw out conflict. This requires discernment. Not all conflicts are potentially productive ones. But often embedded in conflicts are opportunities for learning and important adaptive work. For example, when I came to my current congregation, there was a major conflict going on concerning the endowment and investment policies (precipitated by the issue of divestment in support of the South African anti-apartheid movement). After we had sorted through and resolved that issue, the conflict lingered: Is it good or bad to have an endowment? How is the money to be used? Who gets to decide? This conflict seemed to me to involve an adaptive challenge. The congregation found itself to have significant and growing financial assets in the endowment. Several hundred thousand in 1960 had become $4.5 million in assets by 1990, and $15 million by 1995. What were the implications of this for the congregation's identity and mission?

We set about providing information about the endowment. We tried to think about it theologically. Where had it come from? Who had contributed to it? What did they have in mind? What is its purpose?

What do the Scriptures have to say about wealth and responsibility? Over time, the congregation came to see the endowment not as a secret or an embarrassment of riches but as a resource for ministry and mission, one through which God was calling the congregation to widen its vision and its sense of the possible. The conflict was drawn out for its potential as an adaptive challenge, as an occasion for learning and growth. Not only has the congregation claimed the endowment as a resource for ministry and mission, but planned giving has also become something in which a whole new generation of church members is now participating.

In identifying adaptive challenges, leaders need to ask the purpose question in order to draw out important conflicts and to look for the gaps. One such gap existed in our congregation in the teaching ministry for adults. The sole continuing adult education program was "The Forum," a weekly event that focused on current social and political issues and was a source of congregational pride and identity. It linked the church and the city, and it brought distinguished speakers and community leaders. Yet attendance was falling off. The Forum and its format seemed to appeal more to those born before World War II than to those born after. This was a gap. Many of those who were either new to the church or were visitors had little or no background in Christian faith or practice. Sure, they were interested in current social and political topics, but they desired "something spiritual"; and they wanted "relationships" and the interaction of groups smaller than the Forum. Gradually, through a process of trial and error, we developed a core curriculum of four tracks: Bible study, theology, spiritual life and practices, and ethics. We also developed a small-group ministry called "Covenant Groups."

Asking these questions — what is our purpose as a church? what are the vital few? — are skills for identifying adaptive challenge. Other skills for identifying adaptive challenges are drawing out conflict and paying attention to the gaps. Once a congregation has identified an adaptive challenge and begun work, it is important to "regulate distress."

Strategy Number Three: Regulating Distress

When you are engaged in adaptive work, there will be distress. There will be resistance, and there will be pain. Those who lead congregations in doing adaptive work should expect trouble. This is not indulging in masochism or encouraging a persecution complex; it is simply being realistic. There were lots of times on Israel's journey through the wilderness toward the Promised Land when the people grumbled and groaned and wanted to go back to Egypt. Change is difficult. And adaptive work is difficult because it involves learning, change, risk, and growth. It is what we want, and it is what we don't want.

More importantly, adaptive work does not occur apart from some distress. If everything is just fine and everyone is happy and content, chances are that little work is getting accomplished. To use one of Ron Heifetz's favorite images, adaptive work is like a pressure cooker. You need some heat for things to cook. But you also need to maintain the holding vessel or the holding environment for things to cook. If there is no heat, nothing happens; if there is too much heat, the top blows off. Leadership involves regulating the distress, keeping the stress at a productive level. You have to have enough stress to keep things cooking without creating so much that the top blows off.

Ministers and congregations have many resources for creating a strong "holding environment" while dealing with adaptive change. Worship can create a holding environment as a congregation is put in touch with sources of power and symbols of strength that transcend the moment. Furthermore, effective ministers have long understood the importance of pastoral work if they are to offer prophetic leadership. Developing and maintaining relationships of trust and care allow a minister to lead a congregation in facing hard questions and challenges. The holding environment can also be strengthened, in the midst of change and adaptive work, by events that celebrate a congregation's history, story, and leading figures.

Beyond these ways of regulating distress as a congregation does its adaptive work, there are three other skills that I have found to be important. One is to sequence and pace adaptive work. Don't overload the agenda; you can't do everything that may need to be done all at once. Pace the work. Plant seeds one year for work that will be done the next. As the work proceeds, make occasional use of the pulpit or other communication opportunities (congregational meetings, annual meetings, and church newsletters) to describe the change and put it in context. All of these are ways of pacing the work and regulating distress.

A related skill is valuing small steps. Big changes do not take place overnight. Typically, churches change and do adaptive work slowly. Leaders need to look for and value small steps. They need to be able to see how small steps are parts of a larger strategy. To return to my example of the endowment, we began with a number of small steps: one was getting key boards and lay leaders involved in learning about endowments in other churches; another was providing information about our particular endowment to the congregation. We learned, in doing so, that the average gift was not, as many supposed, a large one — it was $11,000. The endowment was not the creation of a few wealthy people but of many people of ordinary means that loved and believed in their church. Next we created "The Cornerstone Society," a program for remembering past donors and thanking present donors to the endowment. An annual gathering of the Cornerstone Society became a time for talking about the purpose of the endowment and celebrating it as a resource for mission and ministry.

Another skill for regulating distress is changing by addition rather than subtraction. A particular program or ministry may seem to be less effective than it should be. This was true of the Forum. We added new programs of adult education and small-group ministry rather than eliminating the Forum. Truly ineffective programs or strategies may be eliminated at some point; but doing that up front is but a guaranteed way to galvanize opposition. People are much more likely to let go of something that is no longer needed or effective when they have something new to focus on and embrace.

In the midst of adaptive work, leaders must pay attention to distress and seek to regulate it so that there is enough, but not too much. Strengthening the "holding environment," sequencing and pacing the work, valuing small steps, and changing by addition rather than subtraction have proved to be valuable skills.

Strategy Number Four: Maintain Disciplined Attention

When leaders and a congregation have identified — or begun to identify — the adaptive challenge they face and to engage in the work of learning and change, it is important to stay focused on the work at hand. Threats to such a focus tend to come from two quarters. The first is from congregational leaders themselves who grow impatient or distracted and fail to keep their own attention disciplined. Leaders have to be a bit like a dog with a bone; that is, get a grip on the thing and keep gnawing on it. If you run off to chase a ball or a bird, the congregation is likely to get distracted too. If you leave the bone lying around, someone else will make off with it and manage to bury it.

The other quarter from which threats to focus tend to come is from the congregation who are, in all likelihood, unacknowledged masters of work avoidance. You get going on some core issue that will require learning, change, risk, and growth, and — count on it! — some form of work avoidance will materialize. Among the most popular forms of work avoidance are blaming and scapegoating. Sometimes they place blame on events or persons from the past: "After what happened with Minister X, people were never the same." Sometimes they blame the setting: "We are in a pretty conservative area. You can't expect that a liberal type of church is ever going to thrive." Sometimes they will blame the congregation itself: "These are just not very imaginative or committed people." Popular scapegoats include denominations, clergy, and consultants. "They don't understand us and how we do things here." "She's pushing too hard." At other times work avoidance will come in the form of questioning "the process": "We weren't consulted." "Well, we were consulted, but not the right way."

Still other times, people invent burning issues as either a conscious or subconscious attempt to divert attention from the work at hand. As the congregation I serve was in the process of making the shift from board culture to ministry culture and to a "ministry teams" approach, a group in the congregation came forward pushing an old strategy: they wanted the congregation to set everything else aside while devoting the next year to worship, discussion, study, and prayer on the "issues of creation" — all leading to a vote by which the congregation would declare itself a "Green Church." Ecological issues were, according to members of this group, the overriding and pressing issue of our times, and everyone in the church had to engage this issue. Eventually, the response from the governing board was: "No, not everyone has to engage this issue. There are other equally important issues. All those who feel called to work on theology and ecology, and on creation care, form a ministry team and go to it."

The theme of "creation care" is in itself, of course, important and legitimate. That is what makes some work avoidance strategies especially challenging. The issues — at least on the surface — are valid, even urgent. But they may not be the urgent or even real challenges that this congregation needs to address.

I recently worked with a judicatory that was in the third year of a five-year self-study and strategic planning process. When the body gathered for its annual meeting, there was not a single remark that addressed the substance of the self-study or plan. Rather, the issue had become the cost of the work and the endowment of the judicatory. While these were not wholly unimportant questions, the diversion of attention onto the cost question was, for the most part, a classic illustration of work avoidance. In such a situation, sometimes the best thing leaders can do is deal with the pressing issue (the funding questions) but in such a way that it does not overtake the critical work at the heart of the agenda. In this case, leaders had to work hard to keep attention focused on the adaptive work: the purpose of the judicatory and the capacity of its constituents to engage in the process of learning and change relating to that purpose.

A couple of particular skills are helpful in maintaining disciplined attention. I have found it helpful to encourage periodic development of congregational strategic plans. While these, too, can become a form of work avoidance, if they are successful they chart a course that allows a congregation's leaders to focus available resources. A brief, to-the-point strategic plan can also help a congregation avoid the mile-wide/foot-deep phenomenon. "Yes, that is an important matter, but we'll have to wait on that. We already are working on these three things."

A third skill, persistence, is simple yet not to be underestimated. Many clergy give up too soon. While it probably varies some depending on the size and setting of a congregation, it seems generally to be the case that a clergy person does not really become the pastor of a congregation until he or she has been there about five years. Often it is seven, eight or nine years in a congregation before fruit begins to appear. Moreover, many clergy tend to underestimate the need for creative repetition of key themes. When I began my ministry, I had the very peculiar notion that if I said something once, or at most twice, everyone had heard it and that was enough. As the years have passed, it seems that I have two or three key themes that I keep reworking, repeating, and reframing. Especially if you are engaging people in authentic cultural change, it takes time and experience to get under people's skin and into their hearts and lives.

Persistence is also a significant virtue because those who oppose adaptive work, learning, and change will test the leaders. They will try to determine how committed you really are and how much you will hang in there. When it becomes clear that you are not going to go away, give up, or get mad, the dynamics of a situation do change. None of this is to say that leaders should not pay attention to feedback. Absolutely, they should. They should listen and seek to learn as graciously as possible. But, to recall Edwin Friedman's terms, continue to define your own goals, your sense of calling, and stay true to those.

Strategy Number Five: Give Responsibility Back

My emphasis on the importance of leadership should not be understood to mean that it is all up to the leader or leadership team. It is not — nor can it be. For significant adaptive work and cultural change to be done, the people must own the work and accept responsibility for it. Leaders must learn to give responsibility back. Typically, this is not something leaders do readily or well. Often those who take on leadership are already those who have a high sense of responsibility: they are the kind of people who don't mind work, or a challenge, and who readily volunteer. But there is a shadow side to being so responsible. Leaders often take on too much and then find themselves resenting it. Followers do not grow and become leaders themselves. Those who are leaders have to work at giving responsibility back.

When I began in the ministry, I noticed that a lot of people would come up with ideas, suggestions, and projects. Some were even things they were willing to work on. But often what they were saying was, "The church should do this," which, translated, means "You (Reverend) should do this," or at least "Somebody over there should do it (I'm not about to!)." For a time I fell for this. I would listen, nod, agree, and then take on whatever it was that someone viewed as important. Eventually, the load got so heavy that I collapsed under its weight. Slowly, I learned to give responsibility back. Instead of saying "Yes, that's important, let me work on that and get back to you," I learned to say, "Thanks, but I pretty well have my work and calling identified. I am, however, very interested in helping you discern what God is calling you to do and be, and then supporting you in doing whatever that is."

As an example: when we got hold of the adaptive challenge we faced in developing a teaching ministry for adults, the question I framed and then gave back to the Adult Education Board and congregation was, "What do we think Christians need to know? What do we need to know about the Bible, about the doctrines and history of the church, about ethics, about other faiths?" From that question, people were able to begin the work of mapping out a curriculum for adult Christian education and formation.

The previously described shift from "board culture" to "ministry culture" is one way to give responsibility back. Instead of centralizing all ministry in the clergy or the clergy and a few laity, the church should give the ministry back to the congregation. We want to help you discern your call and gain the skills and resources you need to take it on. But we won't do it for you. Often what happens in "board culture" congregations is that a leadership elite responds to congregational concerns by saying, "We will look into that, make plans for it, see about it, and get back to you. Don't worry, we will keep you posted." The "ministry culture" approach results in a different form of communication: "God has called you to this ministry? Terrific! Go to it, and keep us posted."

Another way to give responsibility back is to avoid the vision trap. These days a lot of people have bought into the idea that leaders are the ones who need to have the vision. So a new minister will often find herself or himself asked, "What is your vision?" It is sometimes wise to give responsibility back at this point by asking questions, by buying time, and by directing attention to the question of purpose. In due time, leaders can — and should — provide the outlines of a vision; but in doing so they must be careful to avoid the implication that the work and answers will all come from them. It will be a partnership, and learning to give responsibility back in measured and manageable doses is a key skill.

Strategy Six: Protect Leadership from Below

Leadership is a partnership of leaders and followers. Good leaders will call forth and enable the leadership gifts of others. Sometimes key leadership in making shifts in congregational culture will not come from designated or elected leaders, or even from a congregation's de facto leaders. Sometimes, when you're doing adaptive work, leadership will come from the outside or below. It may come from a person new to the church; or it may come from someone new on a board or committee. It may come from a teenager or group of teenagers. It may come from a person or persons at the margins of the congregation's power and decision-making structure. Typically, those inside the structure are content with the way things are; but those who have been excluded — or at least not included — may be one's best allies in the work of adaptive and cultural change in a congregation. Designated leaders, such as clergy, need to practice the strategy of protecting those who would lead from below or outside.

There are three particular ways in which I have done this. The first is what I call "counting the yes votes": it means that when a new idea is on the table, you don't necessarily have to put it to a majority vote, nor does the whole group have to be in support. Often an authentically new or risky venture will not get majority support. That may be okay. But count the yes votes. Let those who are enthusiastic and committed go ahead. Don't hold them up, frustrate them, or undermine them by insisting or letting others insist that nothing can happen until everyone buys in. In one congregation I served, one group was very interested in getting involved in refugee sponsorship. Some key leaders in the congregation were diffident or opposed. At least in this case, it was not necessary that everyone, or even a majority, cast yes votes. Counting the yes votes is generally a way of supporting the risk-takers in a congregation, precisely the people you may want to encourage when you are engaged in cultural change.

A related way of protecting leadership from below is to be wary of overvaluing consensus. True consensus is a beautiful thing that some groups with a great deal of time and trust can manage. But often today, when people speak glowingly of consensus, what they mean is something that pressures those who may have a different perspective to fall in line. We are so committed in the churches these days to the avoidance of conflict that we will often do anything to give the appearance of harmony. "We believe in operating by consensus here," announces the long-serving chairperson of the board. Translation: go along with me, or with those of us who have been here the longest. Sometimes consensus means that the long-winded win. They will keep on talking until all the sane people who actually have a life give up and go home. Consensus has a place — just not everyplace.

Another way to protect leadership from below is to charter a new working group for a new venture. While there are exceptions, it is generally true that what established boards and committees do best with new ideas is to say no. There's a reason for this: they have their area of work established; they are organized to do that work, and they know how to do that work. So if something comes along that will require significant change, many groups simply say no. Thus, for example, if I want to encourage a group to lead the congregation in a strategic planning process, I generally do not ask the established governing board or church council to do this. I suggest that they create a new group especially for that purpose.

Likewise, when our church did a major renovation of the sanctuary several years ago, we did not ask one of the existing boards — Worship, Property, or Administration — whether this was something that we should do. Chances are good that, if they had been asked to say yes or no, they would have said no. Instead, we established a new group, a "sanctuary renovation task force." While that group was charged initially with studying the feasibility of the project and making a recommendation to the congregation, they were much more likely to say yes — and to do the necessary work.

Leadership in the midst of adaptive challenge is not easy work, but it is good work. These six strategies, along with the particular skills I have described that are related to them, are reliable ones for leaders who undertake this important work. None of them are foolproof "how-to" steps; every leader will have to assess when it is appropriate to use them, and when it is not. All must be adapted to particular congregational contexts. But the leader who gets to the balcony, spends time identifying the adaptive challenge, works at regulating distress, maintains disciplined attention, gives responsibility back, and protects leadership from below will learn a lot about leadership in the process and will help a congregation make changes in its culture that enable it to thrive in a new time.

Index